Subject:
India

Subject: India

A Semester Abroad

Jennifer Ladd

INTERCULTURAL PRESS, INC.

For information, contact
Intercultural Press, Inc.
P.O. Box 700
Yarmouth, Maine 04096 USA

Library of Congress No. 89-045010
ISBN 0-933662-79-3

Library of Congress Cataloging-in-Publication Data

Ladd, Jennifer, 1952-
　Subject India: a semester abroad/Jennifer Ladd.
　　p. cm.
　Includes bibliographical references.
　ISBN 0-933662-79-3
　1. Foreign study—India.　2. American students—India.
3. India—Description and travel—1981-　I. Title.
LB2376.3I4L33　1989
371.19'62—dc20

$$\text{89-45010}$$
$$\text{CIP}$$

Printed in the United States of America

This book is dedicated to Vijubahen and Ramesh, two souls who have flown beyond.

ACKNOWLEDGMENTS

This book has been a long time in process and therefore there are many people to acknowledge. I would like to thank Deborah Mandelsberg for her support and Jeffrey Cole for the use of his computer and to them both for the use of their house as a work space. Steve Moody and Ann Helwege generously provided their computer and work space as well. I am also grateful to Alan and Andrea Rabinowitz for giving me emotional and physical shelter while writing.

I owe a great deal to Betty Jones and Sharon Stine for being on my thesis committee. I particularly want to express my gratitude to Jeanne Strong-Cvetich, who helped me go over every word, paragraph, page, and chapter. Her ideas and encouragement were invaluable.

Thanks also to the School for International Training College Semester Abroad staff—John Sommer, Hildamarie Hendricks, Eloise Biscoe, Autumn Preble, David Whyte, and Ian Baker, who have been friends along the way.

Thank you to Bob Fuller, Helen Ladd, and Evi Seidman for reading the manuscript and encouraging me. Thank you to Evi Seidman for giving me the love, time and space necessary for finishing this book.

Thanks to David Hoopes and Peggy Pusch and others at the Intercultural Press, who were very helpful editors, reminding me once again of the "elements of style."

Thanks to Nanubhai and Sushilabahen Vankar and Ramesh Shroff, who made life at the Vidyapith fun.

Lastly, I would like to thank the twelve students with whom I spent a good deal of time. I am very grateful for their writings offered here, and have been greatly enriched by our adventures together.

CONTENTS

PROLOGUE

In 1983 I left my job as a kindergarten teacher in Seattle, Washington, and headed off to India to travel for six months by myself. I had been involved with elementary education for the past five years and was ready to explore the world beyond the living universe of the classroom.

Originally, I had been drawn to visit some friends who were working in Sri Lanka with the Sarvodaya movement there, a program which is based on Mahatma Gandhi's idea of "the upliftment of all." In Sri Lanka monks and villagers work together to improve not only physical conditions, but the social conditions of the community as well. Unfortunately, just as I was preparing to leave, Sri Lanka was beset by a series of violent uprisings and massacres, making the area unsafe to travel in at that time. I proceeded on to India to explore what was left of Gandhi's Sarvodaya movement there.

My interest in the Sarvodaya movement stemmed from my long-term interest in grassroots organizing in the United States, coupled with a growing need to acknowledge and explore my own spirituality. India appeared to offer an opportunity to meet people who were living the active, goal-oriented life of social change while maintaining the quiet inner life and detachment cultivated by the study of Hinduism and Buddhism. I wanted to understand better how people managed the "doing" world and the "being" world at the same time.

Studying the vitality of the Gandhian Sarvodaya movement was my stated purpose. My unstated purpose (except to a few close friends) was to shake myself up, to expose myself to a totally different world outside the classroom. I wanted to test myself in the waters of the unknown. What would be my response to the poverty? Could I manage traveling alone? How would I react to such a dramatic break in my career?

And so off I went, equipped with a small backpack, some names and a heart full of hopes and fears. Six months later I had traveled all over India, seldom staying in hotels but rather being invited to stay in homes and institutional guest houses. I had been to all-India Sarvodaya meetings, women's meetings, stayed with people who had lived and worked with Gandhi and who were still active. I learned to be open, to trust that I would be assisted, to be comfortable with hours on a train or bus simply looking out the window, watching the towns go by. I also met a wide variety of Indians. I liked some and not others. I grew to enjoy India's contrasts—highly spiritual and rampantly corrupt, extremely vibrant and painfully poor, stunningly beautiful as well as disturbingly ugly. Most important, I found "family"—people that I loved. Through them I entered at least some part of Indian society that I might not have seen had I remained a tourist.

I came back wanting to share the experience with others, wanting to take others on a journey into a confusing and mystifying place. I wanted to see others expand as I felt I had. Three months after my return to the United States I was offered a job by the School for International Training as academic director of a college semester abroad program to India. I gladly accepted and have subsequently written this account of our adventures and discoveries.

There were two semesters, fall and spring. The first semester I had eight students, the second, four. Although

I make reference to those different semesters, the account is basically a composite picture of the two trips. The quotes from students were taken from writing done throughout the semester, except for the orientation discussion, which is based on notes I took during the session. To ensure confidentiality I have changed all the names of the students and of the permanent staff on the Indian campus.

1

THE BEGINNING

The Journey

The day of departure arrives. It's going to be a long haul. The Greyhound buses will come to take students and academic directors headed for Kenya, Nepal, and India to JFK Airport in New York City. We will start at 10:00 A.M. Saturday, leave the United States at 8:00 P.M., arrive in London at 7:00 A.M., fly for ten more hours to Delhi (where we drop the Nepal group), go to Bombay (arriving at 1:00 A.M. Monday), transfer to the domestic airport, and wait for our 6:00 A.M. flight to Ahmedabad, where we will arrive at approximately 7:30 A.M.

Along the way we encounter bits and pieces of the culture. We are flying Air India, are served Indian meals, view Hindi films, are surrounded by women in saris and dark-haired men with moustaches. There is the sound of a number of Indian languages all around. As we circle Delhi we look out the windows with bloodshot eyes, trying to see more than we can see, aching to somehow touch India. The Nepal group deplanes—they are a larger group; we feel abandoned.

It's only us now at the beginning of our adventure together. There are another three hours to Bombay; we sleep fitfully.

Susan and Penny have developed a closeness already, and they strike up a conversation with a man who works with computers in Bangalore. Susan explores the possibility of doing an internship with him after the program since she has taken a year off from school and is planning to stay a full six months. He gives her his address and urges her to write. Her first contact! It's exciting, promising, encouraging. Other students watch with a bit of envy at her ability to jump in and connect. She has also had practice; she has spent time with her relatives who live in Ireland, and she attended high school in France for two years, where she learned French and became accomplished at meeting people of different cultures.

Finally, we reach Bombay and deplane. We are assaulted by a melee of smells: airplane exhaust, cow dung, human excrement, flowers, earth, wood smoke, and cooking—though it is long past supper time and way before *nasto* (breakfast). Along with the Indian fragrance comes the warmth and humidity of coastal air. For students coming from a cold Vermont, the warmth is a doorway to relaxed muscles, a release into a different season, although it is becoming winter in the subcontinent also.

We walk down steps, make our way through disembarkation, passport inspection, baggage collection, customs, the foreign exchange bureau to change our dollars into rupees, and finally we catch the domestic airport bus.

Along the way we encounter a crowd of young men who are interested in carrying our luggage, pushing our baggage cart, and only after the task is completed does the plea for a small fee come! It's late, we've been en route for at least twenty-eight hours. We're exhausted. This onslaught of demanding hands and pleading eyes is difficult to cope with. Robin distributes rupees, feeling sorry for the boys and yet aware of the endless need. There are more hands and more hands and still more hands. The door closes, and we ride through the outskirts of Bombay. The streets are relatively quiet, not many people are out, but we see the array of houses, huts, and shacks that line the road. At our destination, the domestic airport, we unload and wait for our next flight. I find we are not on the flight list—our first bureaucratic challenge. Soon the problem is cleared up; we get in line, check our luggage, board, and doze for an hour, looking out the window at brown and green fields below. At last we get to Ahmedabad and are greeted by our hosts, Rajendra, Narayan, and Sanjaybhai. From my journal:

> We stepped into the Matador van and rumbled out into the countryside, encountering donkeys, water buffaloes, goats, pigs, cows, dogs, camels, women with brass vessels on their heads, men with turbans on their heads, children with matted hair playing in the dirt, fields of green wheat and brown mustard seed ready to be harvested. Auto rickshaws (three-wheeled, covered scooters) barely sidle around us. Bicycles, tractors, scooters, trucks, buses, and jeeps swerve as they meet us traveling down the road towards the village of Sadra, where we'll soon reach the rural campus of the Gujarat Vidyapith.
>
> The students remind me of photographers watching film that is developing; images form before their eyes. They can hardly believe they're in India, even though they are soon sitting on the floor and eating with fingers off round steel *thalis*, surrounded by young men wrapped in blankets, who stare as they chew.

The Program

This was the first of the two three-and-one-half-month semesters I spent supervising American college students in a college semester abroad program in India. The seven months were a multidimensional experience for me, as this report will confirm. The purpose was to "promote cross-cultural awareness and fulfillment of individual developmental potentials that seek to achieve the overall goal of peace and understanding in today's interdependent world."[1]

The students spent three and one-half months in India and followed an academic program that was organized in conjunction with a local university—in our case, the Gujarat Vidyapith, based in the city of Ahmedabad in the western state of Gujarat (see map on page 159).

The Gujarat Vidyapith was founded by Mahatma Gandhi in 1920. It has three campuses: there is the original site in Ahmedabad that is presently for graduate students, both men and women, and then two undergraduate programs for men and women, separately located in two villages, Sadra and Randheja, within an hour's car ride from Ahmedabad. We attended the men's campus in the village of Sadra. For both semesters our schedule was roughly as follows:

Five days of orientation in the U.S.A.

Three weeks at the village campus in Sadra, primarily learning Gujarati, visiting people in the surrounding area and attending classes: the Life and Culture Seminar and the Methods and Techniques in Field Study, taught by the academic director and faculty at the Vidyapith.[2]

Four weeks based in Ahmedabad, completing both of these classes and going on field trips to tribal communities and to the Anand Agricultural University.

Four weeks of independent study, still using Ahmedabad as a base. Students could travel anywhere in Gujarat to conduct research that would lead to a final project.

Two weeks of homestay in another part of India. In the fall we were in Jodhpur, Rajasthan; in the spring we were in Pune, Maharashtra.

Five days of wrap-up and evaluation in New Delhi

before departure. Students were encouraged to remain after the program in order to explore further the vast expanse of India.

By the end of the program students had been exposed to a wide range of lifestyles, economic conditions, castes, and perspectives, with a particular emphasis on rural development.

Orientation: Hopes and Fears

These were students who had chosen India over the familiarity and proximity of France, England, or Germany. They were, for the most part, twenty years old, enrolled in both Ivy League universities and community colleges. They were white, middle-class students from all over the United States. Many had traveled before, but few to a Third World country so far away from home.

During orientation in Vermont, one of the most important sessions was about the students' hopes, fears, and goals. The purpose of this session was to frame the journey. These hopes and fears were the basis for learning objectives, for personal goals. They were also the articulation of the students' awareness of their present limitations and the expression of their desire to expand beyond those limits. This session was meant to expose and make conscious the wellspring from which other behaviors, actions, reactions would flow.

The first night we were all together in Vermont, Margaret read aloud to the group her required essay about why she wanted to go to India. Then the other students read theirs. They were nervous, excited, and polite to one another.

I begin to write this, knowing that in less than two weeks I'll be stepping off a plane into the midst of the most soul-shaping adventure of my life to date. Immediately, my stomach jumps into my mouth—perhaps that is the reason why I want to go to India.... I have seen neither a corpse nor a starving child before in my little bubble world of Joe-college-student U.S.A.; I have never been approached by beggars; praying with my fellow students is not the first thing I'm accustomed to doing every morning; and I can't remember ever taking a shit without taking for granted the availability of T.P. I know the odds are pretty good I'll be intimately confronted with all these things and others I cannot yet guess at, and I know I'll not be able to step back on the plane as the same person who stepped off. I want to explore both inwardly and outwardly, change and grow (hopefully, please, in a positive, sensitive, aware way!), think and see things that might otherwise have remained clouded. I'd like India to be a metaphysical mirror for myself and my "place" in this world.

We sat in a circle; there was a map of India on the wall, incense was burning, the scene was set. In the fall, the group began by first writing out their hopes and fears and discussing them, looking first at hopes, then at fears. In the spring group I asked each student to write an essay before coming. They each read these aloud and talked a little about their background, what they were interested in studying, and why they had chosen to go to India. The following excerpts sum up the thoughts and feelings of the students in both the fall and spring meetings.

The preparation for overseas living, thus far, has been overwhelming to me. What for most vacationers is just a telephone call to a travel agent or getting a vaccination from a doctor is for me a long, confusing, complicated process of organizing, mailing, researching, and pondering. My overall feeling of anticipation cannot be described. India fascinates me. The academic program challenges me. My international and American classmates intrigue me. My personal strength empowers me.

However, just as intense are my feelings of fear, apprehension, minor unpreparedness, and insecurity.

Thus spoke Geoff, an English major from California who had decided to take the year off in order to explore India and, later on, Bali. He had just sold many of his things, vacated his apartment, and embarked on a journey far from friends and family.

Ed was an ardent Reagan supporter, coming to India to see what life in part of the Third World is like, and also because he was an admirer of Mahatma Gandhi and wanted to learn more about him, his ethics and goals.

Daniel came as a religion major, hungry for the mystical and yet strongly attached to his own culture—American music, TV, movies—and quite pragmatic in his outlook.

I'm a little embarrassed about saying this, coming from my Ivy League college, but I hope to find a Holy Man. Maybe not in that form, but I've felt drawn to India since I was thirteen, I'm looking for a wise person, an enlightened soul, or at least, I hope to better understand what that is all about. I want to be able to be idealistic in a practical sense.

Margaret, also a world religions major, came from a small college in New England. She, too, wanted to explore the spiritual realms of India. She wrote:

I'd like to experience a culture embedded in an Eastern philosophical perspective in order to lend some reality to all the textbooks I have been merrily digesting in the name of "higher education." I want to see Krishna, Lakshmi, and Hanuman for myself.

Tania, on the other hand, had come interested in politics and social change:

I've been involved in social issues since high school. I'm interested in seeing what life is like in India and what kind of change is happening, but I'm also hoping to learn more about my own motivations for these interests.

Robin, too, was interested in the lives of the Indian people:

As a child I lived in Kabul, Afghanistan, and I traveled extensively throughout Asia. I can remember the streets of Calcutta, where I witnessed wide-eyed, potbellied children, along with skeletal cattle sharing the pavement. Ever since I left India I have wanted to return. In addition, I have always held steadfast to the ideal that I am Peace Corps material. Perhaps I still have doubts. Before I plunge into a two-year commitment I need a trial period. I need to know that my expectations and career choices are not just part of a fairy tale. If the harsh reality of living in a Third World country is not for me, then I want to come to the realization now.

Eric had also visited India. During high school he and some classmates had done a whirlwind tour of the major cities. He was returning to explore the culture more deeply, hoping to get to know the people, not just the historical sites.

Al was running from a world of family conflict and criticism, from an unchallenging university situation, from a social pattern that was superficial, unproductive, and perhaps self-destructive. I think he hoped that India would change him dramatically, hoped that he could live the magic that he searched for constantly while reading *Dune* and Carlos Castaneda's books:

I'm going to India because I want to see something different. I want to change. I've been in a kind of rut— partying, drinking, fooling around. I'm almost looking forward to the discipline at the Gujarat Vidyapith. I also hope I can come back clearer on my future: I hope I know what I want to do with the rest of college. It has gotten pretty meaningless for me now.

"I, on the other hand, am a little afraid of changing," said Cindy, an anthropology student from California:

> I worry about not being able to talk with my friends when I get back, particularly my boyfriend. It's going to feel strange that their lives have gone on without me.

Cindy had come to have some time away from her boyfriend, to reestablish her sense of self, to go adventuring and exploring.

Penny lived in New York City and had grown up in a wealthy suburb of New York. She had just come from a summer trip to Haiti. She wanted to see more, experience more, expand her horizons, be adventurous, perhaps get some further insight into her life's direction.

Susan and Angela, both from northeast Ivy League colleges, had made firm career choices. They wanted to expand their own world views. Susan hoped to explore a lifestyle different from working twelve hours a day at a computer, both in school and at a job. Angela came as a European medieval history major who had made Sri Lankan and Pakistani friends at college. She wanted to know more to better communicate with them; she wanted to be closer to their cultures, to go beyond the Greek borders of Western civilization.

By listening to others the group members developed trust in one another to the degree that each was able to dig deep or reach high and share. The interchange built bonds of willingness to be open and vulnerable. It also lifted this experience from a potentially narrow academic framework into a larger context that included learning on all levels.

As our conversation continued, students began to express their fears as well as their hopes:

> I'm worried about how Indians see Americans. In England I found a lot of anti-American sentiment; I wonder if it'll be like that in India.

I think if we really immerse ourselves in the culture, learn Gujarati very well, wear *khadi*, make *chapatis*, try out being other than American, Indians may respect us for trying.

I don't think you can really do that. We're wearing our American lenses and we can't really take them off. As Americans there are limitations in terms of how deeply we can be integrated into Indian culture.

I hope they'll see me as an individual, not just as an American.

"What else are people afraid of?" I asked.

Getting sick ... Getting bored ... Being stereotyped and closed off because of being American ... Not getting my act together on my Independent Study Project ... Not being liked by others in the group ... Getting stared at ... Sticking out ... Closing up ... Not being open ... Not taking advantage of every opportunity that comes along ... Feeling powerless.

I responded:

Well, it's very likely that all your fears will come true in small doses. Chances are you will get sick at least once, will get bored, stereotyped, stared at, feel shut down and out of control. This is part of the ups and downs of bumping into another culture, India in particular.

Chances are also high that many of your hopes will come to fruition, or at least they'll lead you to further questions, discoveries, and hopefully fulfilling experiences.

The students then asked me about my hopes and fears.

Well, I hope you all have alchemical experiences (yes, I did use that word)—I hope you learn the art of turning a difficulty into a learning experience. I hope we have many "ahas," both about our own culture and India.

I hope no one gets terribly sick, that the group doesn't get nasty on me, that I can be helpful to you all, that I'm academically rigorous enough, that the rigidity of the Gujarat Vidyapith is not too oppressive, that we have great adventures, see and experience much and come away changed, enriched, wiser, connected with Indian friends, and clearer about our places in the world.

I, too, had some expectations, some mission to see that these students crack their molds, fall out of themselves, become disoriented and then reorganize themselves into more complex organisms, more conscious human beings.

A high order, no doubt, and perhaps an unfair one. As mentioned before, I had just returned from six months of traveling alone in India, where I had visited a variety of Gandhian schools and small village industry projects in remote areas, all across the country. I, in fact, had gone to India for many of the same reasons that the students had just expressed. I had experienced a transformation; India had become a part of me. I wanted to guide these students through a similarly transformational journey, whatever that might be for them.

The hopes and fears that were expressed during that evening session spoke to the boundaries of our own cultures, the stereotypes we had of India and Indians, and revealed the relatively high degree of, at least, intellectual awareness of being culture bound.

Everyone had deep personal reasons for going. There was the consistent search for differences in culture and lifestyle, for confrontation with themselves, and for dislodging themselves from the known and hurling themselves into the unknown. I remember being impressed and pleased with both groups, amazed that they were so aware of wanting to change, knowing that it might be difficult, yet looking forward to it all the same.

In both cases students came away from this first meeting excited, elevated, closer to one another and ready to plunge, and even impatient with the rest of the week's preparations. Adrenaline and energy were tapped as students felt they'd be in touch with deeper parts of themselves and the world as a result of this sojourn into a very different culture.

Another aspect of predeparture preparation was getting background on Gandhi—his life and the movement that arose around him. We saw the film *Gandhi* and read his autobiography. We discussed both the film and the book and outlined the main ideals for which he stood.

The discussion led to a review of the movement following Mahatma Gandhi's death, with a specific look at the Gujarat Vidyapith, which was founded by Gandhi in 1920. At this point we used a letter of introduction to the students from the Gujarat Vidyapith:

> Welcome to the Gujarat Vidyapith. This institution strives to work for Education through Gandhian way of life with the object of contributing to the emergence of a new society based on Philosophy and Practice of Ahimsa (non-violence).
>
> Everything here may be "new and different" to you—bath facilities, food, time-schedules, communications, transport, dress, home-life, social behaviour. All these areas of daily life will need considerable adjustment on your part. Depending upon your individual ability, values of your life and your own experience, the adjustment may be minor or major.
>
> The CSA (College Semester Abroad) programme here may not be as easy, because you have to fulfill your academic requirements while coping with many cultural factors and their impact upon your daily life. In many ways this joint enterprise of Gujarat Vidyapith and your American institution is unique and will need a good degree of patience, a spirit of understanding and forbearance.
>
> The Gujarat Vidyapith has long and unique academic

traditions. Tradition means a great deal to us. We are not enamoured of change for the sake of change. Our dress, diet, and social code reflect the traditions of our institutional life and also of the Indian Culture.

Our hope is that you will constructively explore the issues like the role of Gandhian educational institutions in the development of the rural society and weaker sections of our people in general, and how they are struggling to forge the Gandhian ideas of social uplift and its interactions with other types of ideas.

There is often a tug-of-war between the attractions of city and the discipline of our campus life. You will also experience this. We will be happy to help you to take advantage of the social and cultural resources of Ahmedabad and surrounding districts, however, it should be remembered that the major thrust of the Vidyapith is to work for the uplift of the rural society. It is not easy to comprehend the Gandhian way of life unless you experience it yourself in all its facets. A full exposition of the life here is necessary for all students. This is unlike other universities where there is very little corporate life.

The students were looking forward to the discipline, particularly Al, who felt he needed some limits. They were looking forward to learning more about Gandhi, his ideas and his accomplishments, and to discovering what he means to Indians in modern-day India.

Gandhi took vows espousing freedom of religion, abolition of untouchability, noncooperation with one's oppressors (not buying English fabric—thus the importance of hand-spinning and weaving), self-reliance (the building up of India's resources), and of course truth and nonviolence or *satyagraha* (the ultimate in listening to one's conscience and acting accordingly, never at any point hurting another being). Gandhi required all those who lived in the *ashram*, a school for study, retreat, and meditation, to also take these vows. Today, thirty-seven years after independence and thirty-six years after Gandhi's death, much of the fire of these convictions has died down, particularly as the day-to-day concerns of running a large institution have begun to take precedence.

Being a student at the Gujarat Vidyapith means one generally follows these rules:

1. Wear homespun, handwoven cotton fabric, known as *khadi.*

2. Participate in daily prayer.

3. Participate in daily community spinning.

4. Eat a vegetarian diet (no eggs).

5. Participate in community life, i.e., cleaning, cooking, or working in the fields.

6. Be back at the hostel by 10:00 P.M.

7. Do not invite guests or visitors to your hostel room (to prevent the possibility of theft).

8. Do not smoke in public.

9. Keep separate accommodations for males and females.

10. Clean your rooms, toilets, dishes.

11. Do not accept individual invitations directly since that invariably disturbs group planning.

12. Accept invitations to eat in restaurants only after consultation with the Coordinator on the advisability of eating in a particular restaurant.

During this part of the orientation it was important to keep a delicate balance between warning the students about a system they might experience as rigid and yet not predetermining their reactions. In the recent past, students had been particularly sensitive to this rigidity, to the extent that some problems and misunderstandings arose. The challenge here was to understand the Vidyapith's rules and regulations in their own context of adherence to Gandhi's ashram vows and to better understand the dynamics of crystallization that can occur after the death of a persuasive creator, whose ideas have taken particular forms. Often the forms remain while the spirit is lost.

By the end of the orientation the students had gotten to know one another a little better; they had met with me individually, and we had gone over the academic expectations and requirements. We had generated a high level of energy that propelled us through our journey to the village of Sadra, where we would stay for three weeks.

Sadra

We were housed in the upper story of the guest hostel on the Gujarat Vidyapith rural campus, the Mahadev Grama Seva Mahavidyalay. It was located on the outskirts of Sadra, a village of two thousand people. The area was surrounded by fields of growing wheat, castor beans, millet, mustard seed and cotton. There were also some orchards of guavas, *cheecus*, lemons, and bananas. Many people had water buffaloes for milk and bullocks for ploughing. The campus was on the site of a one-time British agent's estate. The main building was the old mansion. New brick buildings had grown up around it to provide housing for students, staff and their families.

There were about 150 male undergraduates from tribal and low-caste families. They studied agriculture, animal husbandry, spinning, Hindi, English, Gandhian philosophy, and economics. There was one woman on the staff who not only taught Hindi but was also a published Gujarati poet. The director of the institution, Motobhai, was our main guide, friend, and Gujarati teacher.

Our schedule contrasted somewhat with that of the Indian students. They rose at 5:00, attended morning prayer at 5:30, ate at 6:30, worked in the fields from 7:00 to 10:00, and ate a large lunch at 10:30. Then there were classes from 1:00 to 4:00 in the afternoon. Later, they helped with cooking and cleaning, and a few led adult literacy classes at 8:00, after the last communal prayer session at 7:00.

We, on the other hand, had breakfast at 7:30 and language from 8:00 to 11:30. We joined the Vidyapith students in prayer and spinning, followed by further language or free time. The afternoons were spent visiting village craftspeople, both in Sadra and the surrounding villages. We spent evenings either in group meetings, with Motobhai and his family singing and telling stories, participating in local folk dancing, or just having time to ourselves.

We had all our meals alone except for the Indian students whose duty it was to serve us. This was our first encounter with the multifaceted relationship we had with the students. The American students had come to study at the Vidyapith just as the Indian students had, but we were also their guests, which meant that it was their duty to go out of their way to meet our every need. We did not do the same thing for them. This interaction, however, was the locus for most communication, exploration, and play. These students were our teachers, the source of both irritations and gratifications.

We also followed the general mandate to wear khadi. We washed our own clothes by hand, pounding away at them. We used Indian toilets—no seats, just a hole in the floor. Most of the students decided to go Indian-style, using water instead of toilet paper. We ate sitting on the floor, studied on cushions on the floor, and slept on hard wooden cots with a thin cotton pad as a mattress. We had mosquito nets, occasional electricity, and cold running water. To say the least, the students were leading very different lifestyles from their accustomed ones.

Culture Shock

The scene is set, the characters are outlined. What happens next? You may ask, "Don't the students experience some kind of dislocation, disorientation, and difficult times because of all these differences—some kind of culture shock ?" Yes, they do, but not quite the way they expect to.

What is meant by culture shock? Kalvero Oberg originally created the term in his description of the stages that people go through when entering another culture.

> Culture shock is precipitated by the anxiety that results from losing all our familiar signs and symbols of social intercourse. These signs or cues include the thousand and one ways in which we orient ourselves to the situations of daily life.... These cues which may be words, gestures, facial expressions, customs, or norms are acquired by all of us in the course of growing up and are as much a part of our culture as the language we speak or the beliefs we accept. All of us depend for our peace of mind and our efficiency on hundreds of these cues, most of which we do not carry on the level of conscious awareness.[3]

Oberg describes four stages of adjustment. In the first stage the newcomer is fascinated and absorbed, ecstatic and excited by what he or she experiences. In the second stage the newcomer becomes disenchanted, encounters problems, frustrations, and difficulties, and grows to dislike the people of the host country and tends to blame all his/her difficulties on host nationals. During the third stage a sense of humor develops and, Oberg says, there is an increasing ability to use the language and to make one's way around, accompanied by feelings of expertise and a tinge of superiority. In the fourth stage the visitor has grown accustomed to these once-foreign ways and has learned to live in a degree of comfort and enjoyment in which host nationals play a part:

> The environment does not change. What has changed is your attitude towards it. Somehow it no longer troubles you; you no longer project your discomforts onto the people of the host country and their ways.[4]

This is a simple enough format, but what does it really mean? What is really occurring in this process? Peter Adler says, "Culture shock is an experience of personality in culture.... It is an experience in self-understanding and change."[5] It has everything to do with identity; it is the groping for meaning of self in a new context, where many previous cues are replaced by an entirely new set of expectations, assumptions, roles, rules of behavior, beliefs. It is the continual process of surviving, accepting, connecting, and understanding.

From the beginning the students were engaged in a consistent process of extending out, experiencing, and drawing inward—a process like breathing. I think of barnacles reaching out to grasp food, then retracting and digesting. The digestion does not just feed the organism but changes it, so when it once again reaches out it is slightly altered by its last excursion. Each student came with an identity, a conception of self to be tested in Indian cultural waters. Each came with different strengths and weaknesses, with different life-directing motivations, and with different areas of confusion and questions. They also came at different points in their own development: some were self-absorbed, while others had a more expanded sense of self. Some were able to look out beyond the immediate satisfaction of their own needs to see the needs of others. They came with different ways of understanding the world around them.

They were constantly fluctuating between acting for their own safety or towards their own growth, as Abraham

Maslow describes,[6] making choices based on fear or on love. They were continually exploring the limits of their comfort zones, their limits of absorption, the edges of their learning parameters. They were building a *home* within themselves, to which they could once again retreat. *Home* was not necessarily a place but perhaps a way of responding that was familiar, a way of meeting the world that had worked in their previous home-country contexts. They would physically and psychologically travel out into a land of differences, experience them, work and play with them, and then retreat to the familiar once the barrage of stimuli became too complex, disorienting, and unbalancing.

Some students, however, managed to be turtle- or snail-like, carrying *home* with them in their own ability to shift attitudes or interpret situations that enabled them, for instance, to understand the multitude of stares as the genuine curiosity of people encountering a new phenomenon. They were able to identify and empathize with the Indians' experience of them as foreigners and to overcome the feeling that they were being seen as objects. Some found *home* in the back-and-forth exchange with their surroundings. They learned that in allowing themselves to be vulnerable and receptive to, for instance, learning how to milk a cow, they could, in return, receive an open-armed, beaming welcome that could feel as heart- and hearth-warming as any fire in a living room on a cold night.

The process is very complex. Not only does one need to find a *home*, a way of procuring sustenance, but the person who needs sustenance is also changing. *Who am I?* is a question of utmost concern to these students entering India. The usual props for one's self-definition are not there. One is left with the way one asks questions, the way one makes sense of the unknown, and the way one finds psychic paraphernalia to quickly clothe oneself so as not to be so naked, so vulnerable. Robert Kegan describes this process:

> The process of differentiation, creating the possibility of integration, brings into being the lifelong theme of finding and losing.... I am suggesting that the source of our emotions is the phenomenological experience of evolving—of defending, surrendering, and reconstructing a center—which from the view of the developing organism, amounts to the loss of its very organization.[7]

When entering a new culture[8] there are different aspects of identity that become highlighted and may need redefining, such as being an American and, within that, being white, middle- or upper-class, male or female, twenty years old, a college student from a particular family matrix, from a particular geographical location, with particular skills, interests, goals, and confusions.

The sojourn in India was in many ways about this redefining of identity and all that that means, through the vehicles of living with Indians, talking, laughing, negotiating, interacting, and learning more of the Gandhian movement. It was the process of asking and answering questions that were sometimes conscious, sometimes only perceivable through actions and choices.

This process happens throughout life. It can be accentuated and raised to awareness, or thrown into relief by changes in time and space relationships. It is like taking a red design from a red background and placing it on green; the design becomes highlighted. Or as Kegan puts it: the student who is embedded in a particular culture becomes disembedded, becomes aware of distinctions not perceived before and, as a result, grows in his or her awareness of the cultural backdrop, which then allows for the possibility of other colors, other backdrops, other cultural realities.

> The process of movement is plausibly the evolutionary motion of differentiation (or emergence from embeddedness) and reintegration (reflection to, rather than embeddedness in, the world).[9]

These twelve students were coming from the U.S.A., and within that, from a multitude of subcultures, depending on race and ethnic or national background with which they also identified. They came with a set of expectations about the people they would be meeting, both of Indians at large and of Gandhians in particular.

Students' images came from information they had heard, seen, and read in *National Geographic* articles; TV serials like *Jewel in the Crown;* and movies, such as *Gandhi, Passage to India,* and *The Razor's Edge.* They had gained information from their university classes and, in the cases of Robin and Eric, past brief visits to India. Some of the resulting stereotypes were that Indians were uneducated, poor (but happy), starving, sick, holy, wise, exotic, beautiful, close to nature, religious, caste-dominated, and were from large traditional families. They imagined that all Gandhians would be committed, hopeful, compassionate, honest, full of integrity, and dedicated to social change.

Indians we met also had their expectations of us (that students would simultaneously reinforce and try to change). The Gujarat Vidyapith students' stereotypes were based on previous experience with other American groups, on movies like *Kung Fu, Octopussy, The Empire Strikes Back,* and *Raiders of the Lost Ark.* They were exposed to TV shows like "I Love Lucy," "The Odd Couple," and "Dallas," as well as having had contact with Western tourists. They had also heard stories from relatives living in the States. Some educated Indians had American colleagues, and, on the other side of the spectrum of experience, some rural people had impressions based on their experiences with the British.

As Americans we might be labeled as rich; extravagant; sexually free; unconcerned with family (particularly the elderly, fragile and delicate); unable to cope with dirt, the outdoors, or stress; ignorant about countries other than our own; carnivorous and therefore a bit barbaric (addicted to any number of evils, like drugs and alcohol).

And on the more positive side, Americans were seen as innovative, friendly, open, and free-thinking.

As is the case with most stereotypes, there was a grain, if not a handful, of truth in these. Throughout both semesters the students worked to go beyond these stereotypes, learning to understand the intrinsic logic behind behavior or belief that we found strange. As their mental constructs got dismantled, they either replaced them with different, more rigid ones or became more fluid, flexible, or dialectical in their thinking, rarely coming to rest at a final judgment or declaration. The temptation to know, to be an authority based on one's experience is strong, but as Eric said once, "The more we know, the more we don't know. Our experience opens up new mysteries and questions." The story of these students was that of their movement among mental constructs as they negotiated the different levels/stages of understanding both *self* and India. Theirs was the story of traveling physically, but more significantly, emotionally, mentally, and psychologically, through India and through their own mental and emotional mazes within that context.

The Learning Process

Working with a model developed by Theodore Gochenour and Anne Janeway, we can view the cross-cultural learning process as divided into seven stages:

1. Establish contact and essential communication.

2. Establish *bona fides* and be accepted (i.e., be acknowledged and allowed to remain in the host culture).

3. Observe what is going on and sort out meaning.

4. Establish a role within the role definitions of the host society.

5. Develop conscious knowledge of self as a center, self as a cultural being and one taking responsibility.

6. Consciously develop needed attributes and skills—mental, emotional, and physical.

7. Derive a self-sustaining and meaningful relationship within the host culture.[10]

As the authors say, these are not distinct stages; they happen simultaneously and with varying degrees of intensity. The students were involved with the first three during these first three weeks in Sadra. There were three different ways through which students met their *selves* and encountered India during our stay—three portals, one might say, through which they entered Indian society. The first portal was our interactions with the Indian students with whom we had the most constant contact. Talking and playing with them became one of the main avenues for learning how to communicate. By the end of the three-week stay the American and G.V. (Gujarat Vidyapith) students had formed friendships with one another, which prompted visits with Indian students and their farming families later on in the semester.

The second portal was exposure to and involvement in Sadra and the surrounding villages. We visited many homes, workshops, schools and farms in the three weeks of our stay. Through this experience the students became increasingly well informed about the realities of village life for a range of castes and communities.

The third portal was learning the Gujarati language and culture. This study in communication not only enabled students to begin to speak the language but also expanded their awareness of the Gujarati way of looking at the world. Throughout this three-week period the students and I continued to have meetings and classes, to live closely together, and to spend most of our time with one another.

The group became a place for processing experiences and forming supportive friendships, a place of reflection and analysis that led to further insight into both American and Indian culture.

Portal One: Interacting with the Indian Students

As the Indian and American students got to know each other, they began to break through their stereotypes. First impressions were not necessarily disproven; instead they were filled out and expanded. For instance, Susan and Penny consciously and energetically engaged themselves with the Indian students. They stayed after dinner, joking and socializing with these young Indian men, who were more than delighted by their company. They listened to tapes, disco-danced, played *Karoum*, laughed and teased one another. Every so often the young women attempted to ask questions about the men's families, about their job possibilities and their marriage plans. The young women enjoyed the company of the men, superficial as it was in content, because they lacked the language and because their life experiences were so different. Susan and Penny didn't want to miss any opportunity to *be in India*. The Indian men enjoyed it too and began feeling more familiar with the women, enjoying their unconstrained laughter, their informality, and their apparent lack of barriers in relating closely to men.

The Gujarat Vidyapith students were not allowed to smoke on campus; therefore, smoking was done surreptitiously. It is also generally considered improper for women to smoke in India. Penny would smoke upstairs in her room. She had wanted to keep this a secret from the men since it would get around campus in a matter of moments and would be a point of teasing, which would push her out of the individual personality that she was slowly developing with the men back into a stereotyped image of an American woman.

Once, when she was smoking, Jagdesh and Galabhai chose not to heed her protestations, and walked in on her. She became very angry, screamed at the men to leave, and physically pushed them out the door.

Her behavior was not only different from the way most Indian women would react but was also different from the way she had been relating previously. Jagdesh pouted for some time afterwards, feeling confused, betrayed, and misled by the familiarity, the flirtation, the friendliness which had led him to believe he could just walk in. He thought the protestations were a part of the game.

Penny, on the other hand, had begun to feel the heavy pressure of being "on" all the time. She was fatigued from continually keeping up a bantering conversation. She already felt a little uncomfortable about her popularity on campus and about being known as one of the women who danced with the men and who was lively and affectionate. She felt uncomfortable with her ever-watching fan club. She didn't want her image further embellished by being caught smoking. Petty as it may seem, the smoking contributed to her being stereotyped as another loose American woman. She wrote:

> I wonder exactly how the Indians feel. Will I be gawked at like the Fat Lady in the circus for my entire stay in India? At home, I always wanted to have some unique quality that would qualify me as being different. Fortunately (or unfortunately), I fit in with everyone else. Now, here I am, trying to fit in but feeling like the Fat Lady.... I realize that my every movement outside this hostel is being observed. And though I don't want to change my behavior, the thought that "all eyes are on me" makes me think twice before I act.

She was in a tangle—she wanted to be herself, but that self contributed to the stereotype. She had lashed out at this kind of labeling, and it was a sobering experience. After this incident she withdrew a bit more, did not spend as much time downstairs interacting with the G.V. students, and began to discriminate more in her choice of whom she would talk with.

This pattern of extending herself energetically and enthusiastically, followed by a rapid retreat to a safe place, then followed by a bit more cautious extension, was a recurring one throughout the semester for Penny (and for others as well).

Penny had said during orientation, "I expect myself to really be able to enjoy all degrees of this trip. I want to be able to participate in almost everything with a good heart." She had wanted to be "herself" and not be too careful about offending Indians, feeling that they should also learn about America by experiencing her.

Stereotyping doesn't allow for the messy, fuzzy edges of human interaction. It is convenient and easy. It is a quick frame of reference in which to stash another human being. Stereotyping is the bulwark and perpetuator of fear and blindness. It is the signal of limitations, of boundaries that prevent the question of one's own true identity. To be stereotyped is to be lumped together, grouped, corralled like beef headed for the slaughterhouse. These kinds of labels are inescapable except through the activity of love, experience, and connection; then the viewer and the viewed may meet and catch a glimpse of themselves in the other. The students were just beginning to discover the confusing dynamics of stereotyping.

Geoff had an experience that illustrated the tenuousness of an emerging friendship beset by the temptation on both sides to revert back to stereotyping.

Geoff had been taking quite a few photos; he always had his large camera and camera bag with him. He had also bought a custom-made, monogrammed silver ring from the local goldsmith. One night after dinner he went to the village's only "hotel" (restaurant) to have a Campa Cola with the guys. As was true everywhere we went, particularly in the rural areas, people always gathered tightly around to stare and see what was happening. This time, somehow, the conversation turned to the United States, and soon Geoff found himself bombarded with accusations about U.S. funding of weapons for Pakistan and sneering questions about how much his father made and how much his watch, camera, and clothes cost. There were snide remarks about rich Americans coming in and flashing their hardware, disapproving grumbles about the high rate of divorce and the number of old people in nursing homes. All of this seemed to Geoff to be a free-for-all exercise of get-the-American. He came away defensive, angry, and upset at being treated like a rich American, and hurt that the G.V. students who had accompanied him had not come to his defense and were sometimes part of the harangue.

He had to sort it all out. He didn't feel rich; he had had to sell his old baseball cards, get a scholarship, and work to come on this trip. Yes, it was true that his family lived in the San Fernando Valley; they did have a pool and he did have his own apartment with all the accouterments (that he had consciously rid himself of before coming to India). He felt stereotyped as a rich American, and so he was in their eyes. He felt the pain of being locked within these images built up from the villagers' experience with other students who had come through, with TV shows, and the reality that they, absolutely, did have less material wealth than most Americans. Geoff was not the only one to experience being evaluated according to his possession of material goods. The American students constantly experienced the pain of this reality; the anger and complementary guilt were an ever-present hum that occasionally rose in decibels, depending on the situation and the students' sensitivity to the issue.

Many Indian students were very interested in the things that the U.S. students had brought: digital watches, small travel clocks, fancy flashlights, cameras, tape recorders, Sony Walkmans and tapes. It was natural for the G.V. students to be curious; they were not allowed to have radios or even irons in their rooms. The American students felt a complex of emotions. They felt embarrassment at the monumental financial gap between themselves and their Indian counterparts. They also felt irritation with the Indian students' focus on material goods. They felt fear and distrust that their items might get stolen. But they also enjoyed sharing their favorite music on the Walkman, being able to take photos of people and giving them the pictures, and tape-recording their songs and playing them back. They enjoyed sharing their gadgets as long as they were not condemned for having them at the same time.

Just as Jagdesh had felt betrayed and misled by Penny, Geoff felt similarly about the two students who had gone with him to town. He had thought they had begun to communicate and to get to know one another. After all, in America the rules were that one doesn't pull away from a friend or acquaintance who is being harassed and join with the crowd that is doing the harassing. The Indian students, however, were not simply friends and acquaintances; they were also our hosts, our servers. Their role was to make us tea, serve us dinner, fix the electricity, boil water, and generally attend to our needs. These activities were part of their duties at the hostel. Although they no doubt enjoyed the American students, they did not come to the situation out of pure good will; they were in a role that inevitably distanced them from their American guests.

Throughout the semester there was an ongoing sorting out about what friendship meant, how duty and friendship were related, what duty entailed, what the duty of the host was, and what was expected of the guest. Our variety of home visits throughout the semester gave us ample opportunity to explore these issues in more depth and constituted the second portal through which the students entered Indian society.

Portal Two: Immersion through Village Visits

During the third week at Sadra, after two weeks of language study and visits in the village, students went off for a weekend visit, each with a different family. This became another opportunity to embark on Gochenour and Janeway's third stage in the process of awareness, to "observe what is going on and sort out meaning." They had begun to see themselves and their culture reflected back to them by their experiences with the Indian students. Now they had a chance for longer contact with Indian families, away from the safety and smothering presence of the group.

Margaret's experience was one of immersion in the life of women in a small village outside of Sadra. The Vidyapith had a dearth of women: our only contact was with Radhabahen, wife of Motobhai, the language teacher, and with Mirabahen, the Hindi professor, whose main love and talent was writing poetry. Otherwise, our contact was solely with men, leaving the students relatively ignorant about the day-to-day rhythms of Indian women's lives. Margaret describes her village visit:

> It is 8:30 in the morning, and I am sitting in the kitchen watching Elka, Rathurbhai's eldest daughter, cut cauliflower into a pot. She squats on the uneven cement with the pot clutched between her toes, singing a Hindi film song to me and chuckling impishly when I attempt to stutter the nonsensical syllables back to her. The knife she uses is badly blunted, but her fingers are strong from infinite hours of practice; the pieces plop gently down with an absent-minded precision. Her dark eyes never leave my face, seemingly oblivious to both cauliflower and knife, and I am amazed that she doesn't slice off a thumb.
>
> I will be spending the next three hours in the kitchen watching Elka fuss about with pots and cow dung patties,

preparing a meal that will take less than fifteen minutes to eat. To my Western eyes, the kitchen more closely resembles a cave: dark and cramped, with dingy grey walls streaked black in places from the smoke and splattered oil of the cooking fire. Two sets of shelves ring opposing sides of the room, heavy with water jars, cooking utensils, two blue Superman thermos bottles, a spice box, some vegetables and bananas delivered earlier by a village vendor, covered dishes of leftovers, toothcleaning powder, and a few flower-patterned cups and saucers for tea. In one corner are a water spigot and accompanying floor drain; in another, a curved pit hollowed into a cement block. Just wide enough to rest a pot in, its mouth belches out unswept ashes and a few still-glowing bits of wood and cow dung patty. There are two small windows latticed with thick metal bars through which the majority of the eye-stinging smoke is sucked out and through which a few renegade birds with hungry eyes flutter in. Plates and pots and forgotten scraps of food are strewn across the floor, creating an edible obstacle course for the black mouse that careens periodically out from under the shelf, around a pot, across Elka's skirt....

The cauliflower is now perfectly and thoroughly dismembered, splashed with water from one of the jars, and set indifferently aside. Elka then plucks up a pan of rice previously hidden in the chaos on the floor. Beginning a new Hindi film song, she sifts quickly through the grains, flicking pebbles, clumps of dirt, and wandering insects onto the floor with fingers still sticky from cauliflower juice. She pauses occasionally to wipe her nose on the corner of her shirttail and to sweep away from her eyes the blue/black strands of hair that have escaped the braid she did not have time to comb this morning.

Bindu (daughter number three) enters quietly to fill up a small plate with rice and vegetables left over from last night's supper. She squats by the water spigot in the corner, pops a preliminary fingerful of the mush into her mouth, slaps on the water, and then sets about scrubbing dirty pots and eating her breakfast simultaneously. The "soap" she uses looks suspiciously like sand—on several occasions I think I hear her rice crunch in her mouth. Bindu is in the eleventh standard, studying "commerce." When asked if she wants to go to college, she becomes very flustered, ducking her head and mumbling, "I don't know yet." When asked if she wants to get married, she says she doesn't like to cook.

Ba, the fat and balding mother of the household, bustles into the kitchen just as Elka is stacking the rice and some yellowish lentils into a pressure cooker. Ba jabbers something unintelligible to the two sisters, who jabber back, and then, with Rajesvari (daughter number four) in tow, Ba stalks out to the adjoining washroom to attack the morning laundry. With Rajesvari pulling at a pump handle that is half a foot longer than herself, Ba soaks the shirts and underwear, smacking them on the cement floor and moaning about the pain in her joints. She asks me if I have a washing machine at my house in America.

The kitchen begins to grow very warm as the heat from the newly kindled fire oozes outwards, the cauliflower pot now humming merrily over the flames. The pressurecooker has been perched atop a kerosene burner, which Elka has to pump every few minutes or so as the blue light underneath sinks. She is busy kneading chapati dough, waiting for the cauliflower to finish steaming so she can slap the paper-thin circles into their pan. She tells me proudly that her husband's house in Ahmedabad has a gas stove and a stand-up kitchen. She was married last May and will finally be joining her husband in another month or so. Unlike Bindu, Elka likes to cook.

Indrajit (older brother number one) pokes his head tim- idly into the kitchen as if afraid to break the magic circle woven around the women's space. He has some pants he wants Elka to mend. With an appraising glance cast over her cauliflower, Elka unfolds herself, brushes the flour from her hands off onto her shirt, and slips off to find her sewing box. Bindu stops her pot-scrubbing for a moment and smiles almost apologetically at me. With the sound of

Ba's slapping laundry in my ears and the sting of Elka's cooking fire smoke in my eyes, I don't even want to think about refrigerators, microwaves, and washing machines.

The village visit enabled the students to deviate even further from their accustomed lives, allowing them a glimpse of the daily patterns of Indian family life they had only seen from the outside. The range of choices available to most Indian women is more limited than those of even Bindu, who might consider college. Marriage is the expected vocation of women, particularly village women. Margaret had read of this before; however, immersing herself in a household of women made her more acutely aware of what that lack of choice meant and how Indian women might experience it.

Angela's village visit gave her an opportunity to "establish *bona fides* and be accepted," and to "observe what is going on and sort out meaning." Her story illustrates another aspect of the responsibility of being a representative of American culture.

The room was small and dark, reached by narrow, ladder-like stairs. It seemed to be a storeroom—grain sacks were piled in one of the corners—but there were two chairs and a rope cot. I was given one of the chairs. The *serpanch* (leader) of the village, when he arrived, was given the other. I was glad that Chaterbhai was there. In the short time I had known him he had become a friend. His sense of humor had made several awkward moments easier, and, although his English was not particularly fluent, he could often catch my meaning faster than Husanbhai.

I glanced out of the window. In the halo of light around a tractor stood a crowd of men, their white clothes brilliant in the darkness. A few minutes ago I had been in the center of that group, isolated, the sole focus of that silent pack. Chaterbhai had released the tension there simply by asking how I felt. "Like a television set," I said. We moved upstairs.

I looked around the storeroom where I now sat. It had filled up with men, most of whom I had met before. They were talking among themselves in Gujarati. I could understand almost none of their conversation. The scene looked like a Rembrandt: dim light, rich browns of their skin, and stark, startling white cloth. When I looked down, my arms seemed to have turned pure milky white, and I realized with a shock how strange I must look to them.

The men began to ask me questions about America. I had been questioned before, but this felt like a meeting of the village elders. Their questions were complicated and required thoughtful answers. I was frustrated by the amount of generalizing I had to do. Often I was not sure if they had really gotten the point of my answer. They would discuss in Gujarati, then fire off another question. They were particularly curious about American technology, standard of living, and prices. I was asked about our national song. I told them that it is called "The Star-Spangled Banner," but that I didn't know it well enough to sing it. The men seemed rather amused as well as surprised that I didn't know my national anthem, and I had a flash of guilt. In a sense I was an ambassador. I was the only firsthand source on America which they could question. It didn't seem to be fair to them not to be able to respond to so basic a request. I hoped they wouldn't decide that I was unpatriotic and therefore an unreliable source, because I was trying to be as honest and complete as possible. The moment passed, however, and the men went on to new questions.

As I sat, looking from face to face, I was surprised at how relaxed I felt at being cross-examined by another group of men. I did not feel isolated as I had earlier while in the center of the crowd down below. I was American, and they were simply curious. I was curious about their response to my answers, so I watched them as they discussed, or looked down at the group still gathered around the tractor. I wondered whether they were discussing me. It did not seem particularly significant either way.

At that moment I fit in. I had a place and a purpose. I wasn't constantly the main focus of attention, yet I was not excluded, either. The quiet voices speaking Gujarati criss-crossed around me. The dim light felt almost like firelight. As a man would turn, his face would come from shadow to light which emphasized the fine-boned features. I felt solid, heavy, as though my blood was cream instead of rich red. As I grew tired, I could feel my mind wander. I asked Husanbhai if we could go, since I knew my answers were becoming hurried and unreliable. I felt a slight resentment that these men would assume I was an authority on America and demand so much of me, and I felt that I owed them honesty and thought.

Angela found a role, a place from which to speak. She was able to step out of herself and see how she might be perceived by those around her, and she could feel, through the potentially uncomfortable form of a ring of strangers, the genuine interest with which these villagers were reaching out to her. She came to trust members of the group and so was able to relax, open her eyes, ears, and mind for authentic exchange. She had achieved the psychic space needed to examine what it means to be an American. She experienced the heaviness of the responsibility of being an ambassador for her country. She became the new stereotype in that village; when people heard of Americans, they thought of her. She sensed the opportunity to expand the horizons of her questioners while, at the same time, expanding her own as she listened for what interested them, watched their reactions, and experienced the tone of her environment.

Daniel also made his way to a small village about ten miles away. He chose to visit with a deeply religious man in the hopes of finding a path to his symbolic Holy Man. He, however, developed a migraine headache, which put him in a vulnerable state, tapping into one of his (and all the students') fears about coming to India: sickness—at what other point does one need home more?

We're sitting on the floor eating lunch, me in my khadi, Dixit in his Brahmin loincloth. I think we're eating pickled mangoes—tastes kind of off-beat, kind of rubber-like.

"So Dixit Sahib. What do they do in India for headaches?" I say it in "Indian" for him: **soo Dix-it-sah-heeb. What doo they do for the head-ache in India?** The habit is automatic, Dixit speaks English fine, probably better than I do.

This time he takes long to answer. Sometimes, when Dixit gets a question that really makes him think, he sits there with his eyes closed and looks like he's going to drop off to sleep right there in front of you, but then he opens his eyes and they're sparkling and he has an answer for you just like you wanted.

"Ah-cha," he says. (In Hindi it means "I see," or its equivalent—a cross between "Gotchya" and "Ah-so.")

"Head-ache," he repeats. "This is caused by *cold* on the head." He points to his head, "In India we rub *ash* from the fire."

"Ash." Oh yes, ash, how nice.

But my head is tilted backwards, swallowing down some water, and it feels like my brain has swelled up twice its size and starts to squeeze on the eyeballs. Squeee-eeeze.

Dixit looks at me, eyes twinkling. "Yes, yes, *ashes.*"

"I see. Fascinating." He nods and mops up the grains of rice with his right thumb and forefinger. But soon it's close to one in the afternoon and the sun's turned up full blast. I'm sitting there on the porch screaming out half-broken English sentences to Dixit's son. "**In America we go to ride....**" Squeee-eee-eeze. "**Do you ... follow ... ride?**" Squeee-eee-eeeze.

Dixit hobbles over, likes to see what's going on. He looks chipmunk-faced, legs thin and poking out below his loincloth.

Squee-ee-eeze.

"Dixitsahib ... I ... have ... headache."

"Ah. Oh! You-you have headache?"

"Ha! Ha!" No joke—*"Ha"* means yes in Gujarati.

"Ah-cha. Ah-cha. You must sleep. Sleep is good." So he puts me to bed. I wake up to the sound of Hindu chants and the cold, sharp clanging of the temple bell. Dixit built a temple next to his house, just like a shed or garage. Tonight there are visitors. Dixit is coming over with another man. They are looking intense and concerned and are talking Gujarati.

"This man can cure your pain," Dixit tells me. I look at his friend. He has dark skin and a deep-set, hard stare. I feel a hand grasp each one of my temples and the grip tightens up hard like a clamp. Then the Hindu prayer begins, mumbled low and fast and monotone beneath the breath. The pain is still there. The man is a faith healer. I am told to have faith. But the pain in my head pulsates harder than ever and I do not care about faith healers and ashes and Krishna and prayer bells. For just a moment, I want the pain to go away. Cultural awareness is swept away like the avatar ascending.

I feel sick to my stomach. No supper that night. Before sleep I shake two Bayer aspirin from the bottle into the palm of my hand. Dixit's face is full of heartfelt concern.

"You take tablets?"

"Right. For headache."

"Ah-cha. Tablets are very bad for the heart." His wife there in her sari is also alarmed. The four children stand around the bed in a circle, alarmed.

"My friend has given me medicine to give you which will ease the pain. You must drink it at sunrise to cure the pain."

Ah-cha.

"What you need now is a foot massage."

Oh shit.

I woke up the next morning before dawn. The rest of the family slept in cots next to mine on the front porch. I looked up at the clouds moving, pink and silent. Past the front gate I saw the dim, dark outlines of distant trees. The land goes on like this for a long, long way, I thought. And nowhere, nowhere in sight is there the clean antiseptic air of an American doctor's office. No tables full of *Smithsonian* magazines and *Reader's Digest*. No nurses with white clean hats. Just miles and miles of field, speckled with small cement and cow dung huts, and the people, and the people, and the people.

The people with their strange, religious health cures. The people with their strange folklore, their simple ways of life. And all of it enmeshed in this flat, endless land. The earth exudes them. I thought, the ground sweats out the mud huts, the people ooze out of the mud huts like insects, crawlers....

And now, head pounding, I am dependent on them, and them alone.

Dixit wakes up now and he sees me there sitting up, arms wrapped around knees.

I concede. He is there to help me, and is genuinely worried. Worried and concerned. Isn't that what chicken soup is all about? I look back at the potion. I look around me again at the distant horizon, now dimly lit. I sit there in the center of the fields and drink the draught. It tastes good, like sugar water.

And America is a long, long way away.

Daniel went through quite a shift here. Although he remained aligned with Western medical care and though this environment was strange, he was able to transcend the need to see his cure coming from chicken soup in a bowl on a table in New Hampshire and was able to see it here in a cup in Gujarat, and to drink it. He began to enter Gochenour and Janeway's fifth stage in the process of cross-cultural awareness—"develop conscious knowledge of self as a center, self as a cultural being and one taking responsibility."[11] He conceded; surmounting his own resistance, he surrendered to the caring that comes through no matter how different the form might be.

Portal Three: Language and Communication

During the course of the three weeks, the students and I studied the Gujarati language with Motobhai as our teacher. The language component, while only introductory, was an integral part of the students' cross-cultural communication training.

As Edward Hall says in *The Silent Language*, culture itself is communication in that culture may be viewed as a continuous process of communicating and reinforcing group norms:

> Communicating well involves more than understanding the word and speech patterns common to the new culture. It requires work in identifying cultural norms, understanding relationships between people as they are understood by host nationals, and understanding people's intentions within a given communication setting.[12]

or, as Penny succinctly said in her evaluation:

> Language means nothing more than communication but communication does not necessarily entail language.

The students never became fluent in Gujarati; the time was too short, they did not live continuously in Gujarati-speaking homes, and often, particularly in Ahmedabad, Indians chose to speak English with us. As Daniel said, "I felt that my language practice was being obstructed by a cultural phenomenon: the Indian host's refusal to inconvenience me by speaking his native tongue." They did,

however, feel that they had learned a lot about communication. Penny said:

> Five years of Passé Composé didn't help me communicate with others as well as those three weeks studying in Sadra. Probably one of the most interesting insights I learned about communicating with Indians came not directly from the blackboard but indirectly from interacting with the other Indian students. The nonverbal communication that I picked up (by way of attempting to use verbal communication) helped me a great deal in understanding the Indians today. If it hadn't been for those three weeks I might have missed a lot of what was going on around me in the form of strange sounds and hand gestures. I'm now a little afraid people at home may think I'm a little weird (or weirder) when I constantly click my teeth together as though I'm about to ride off into the sunset. I understand that thumb to mouth means "I want water," and especially that the stare does not always have that negative feeling it has in the U.S.A.

She went on to relate a time when she felt she had forgotten which language was being used, that she was only conscious of exchanging meaning:

> My big "aha" came when Galabhai and I had an "in-depth" conversation that went beyond "pass me the milk." We talked in sentences half Gujarati and half English. Without even thinking I could invert my English sentences into the syntax of Gujarati style. Though I didn't know all of the necessary vocabulary to express my feelings we really did understand each other by talking backwards.

Angela became particularly involved in the language when she began to translate Mirabahen's Gujarati poetry into English. She said, "I have gotten some concept of the patterns of thought and preconceived ways of regarding the world and one's place in it. It's a question of what there are and are not words for."

During the course of the language study and the Methods and Techniques in Field Study, we discussed the various realms of nonverbal communication. Students began to watch closely and picked up gestures and sounds that indicated "enough," "water," "yes", "no", and "maybe." By the time the village weekend visits rolled around, the students had become very creative in finding ways to communicate.

Geoff's village stay with a Rabari cowherd proved to be quite an exercise in nonverbal communication. The cowherd spoke absolutely no English and this was only Geoff's second week into Gujarati, but both were able to get their meaning across because of the desire to be involved with one another. Geoff writes about his foray into Rabari culture and his efforts to communicate:

> The feeling, as a result of having been taken in by strangers with nothing in common beyond wanting to learn more about one another, is inexpressible. My expectations were few; polish the Gujarati, milk a few cows, learn about the Sap [snake] Temple, and meet my family. Hence what I did was eat, relax, feed water buffalo, mold some cow dung fuel, listen to the sound of old shepherds gossiping, and ring a prayer bell in the temple. I have never experienced such growth facilitated by such a simple existence.

> My identity really changed as I spent time with my father, Mohanbhai. This personal metamorphosis from *vidyathi* (student) to Rabari shepherd was inescapable. There I was, sleeping on my cot on the porch when I was unsettled by a whispered "Govindbhai ... Govindbhai" (Geoff's Indian name). I came out from under the blankets that had been so sensitively placed upon me the night before by Mohanbhai to see him standing in the glare of a single candle, holding a shepherd's shirt and gesturing for me to slip into it. I stood in the cold of the Indian morning and watched Mohanbhai dress me, as my mother did when I was a child attending nursery school.

He carefully fastened each button, tied each string, and fanned the skirt of the shirt so as to make the ruffle stand proudly. He then reached for a rectangular piece of cloth that was to become a pair of pants. He pointed out the maroon embroidery on the corner, "MR" for Mohan Rabari, his father, who had passed them down to his son. I held up the shirt as he made intricate folds and knots in the cotton cloth around my waist. The cloth now fastened securely about me, he reached down at my feet and pulled the bottom of the *lungi*-style dress through my legs and attached the cloth to the back of my waist. With a pat on my back and a shake of my shoulders, Mohanbhai stood a distance back, touched his hands to his face, and said a complimentary word in his native tongue. He then placed a scarlet turban on my head, handed me a shepherd's walking stick, and placed a rainbow-colored rope belt around my waist. As if the clothing was not enough to overwhelm me, Mohanbhai completed this ritual by looking me in the eye and said in his proud tone, "You Govindbhai Rabari, my *dikaro* (son)." *Pitaji* (father), as he gestured to be called, gave me lessons in carrying the walking stick, herding cows, and greeting other Rabaris with the enthusiastic "Ram-Ram" familiar to only their caste. With no doubt, to Mohanbhai or myself, this preparation was for my debut in Sadra's village center. Mohanbhai took my hand and led me toward the village. As we walked he glanced over at me continuously, with a happy grin of such satisfaction and a giggle. He was like a young schoolboy showing off his new clothes on the first day of class, so hopeful everyone would see them and praise him as well. No sooner had we started down the path than I received a pat on the rear, motioning me forward with a warning of a shepherd up ahead. Mohanbhai said in a whisper only I could hear, "Govindbhai, Ram-Ram!" And there I was, off to greet my fellow shepherd. The laughter of these two men filled the pathways as they remarked about my actions which appeared very humorous, while at the same time, were very well received.

As we entered the village, the crowds clustered closely. The community was very surprised and pleased at what had become of the familiar American face. Many people wanted to see us together and they called out our names. Mohanbhai took control by stating an "ek minit" to one shopkeeper as we were dragged into a shop by another. We were offered cigarettes, water, vegetables, tea, and betelnut. We visited, we laughed, we walked, we sat and listened. Mohanbhai continued to refer to me as his son and never did we pass a shepherd without the "Ram-Ram" greeting. Overall, I was very proud to be with Mohanbhai, to be wearing the Rabari clothing, and I felt exceptionally proud to be a member of Mohanbhai's family.

My experience was significant for many reasons. When I first met Mohanbhai, my heart was touched. He was so warm and so funny. I knew he was someone I would like very much and who I would like to befriend more intimately. Inasmuch as we were prevented from wholeheartedly interacting because of the language barrier, we were able to communicate with one another. Language, both English and Gujarati, was secondary and basically meaningless compared to our use of sign language, touching, eye contact, and especially the genuine presence of sincere human emotion. Mohanbhai cares; I care. We both worked at communicating and we both achieved a meaningful relationship.

As I stood on the roadside next to Mohanbhai, just prior to departing from his small farm, I had an overwhelming feeling of emptiness consume me. I really began to miss him and to long for the moments we shared ... which were now memories. Mohanbhai embraced me and said, "Govindbhai Rabari, my son." My heart pounds, my eyes weep. My life changes.

Geoff entered this situation ready to take on the role of Rabari totally, although only for a short time. He put himself in a position that most of the other students would have shied away from for fear of looking foolish; it would be too hard for them to give up their identities so completely in such a short time. Even though the Rabari role was superficial, Geoff became much more aware of what Mohanbhai's life was like than he would have otherwise. He also had an opportunity to ameliorate his own discomfort with being the American who had been so forcefully attacked earlier in the restaurant. He embraced the family in which he stayed; he was willing to be one of them.[13]

If Geoff had taken on this role for the whole time we were in India, if he had discarded his own cultural personality and taken on that of an Indian, this sojourn into the Rabari community could be called what David Hoopes[14] and other students of cross-cultural experience have termed "going native," which constitutes a kind of escape from the demands of effective adaptation. For Geoff this was more of a balancing experience to round out his other encounters with both the village people and the Indian students. Communication here consisted of learning to wear the clothing, carrying the walking stick, and behaving in a manner appropriate to Rabaris. His willingness to join the family, to give recognition to this community was in a way a gift that he gave; Mohanbhai in return invited Geoff to be involved and offered the warmth of temporary fatherhood.

Geoff had easily taken on Mohanbhai's life. It was fun, interesting, and resulted in a satisfying bonding. Others were not so quick to pull on the clothes of their Indian host families, either literally or figuratively. They felt uncomfortable donning the outward symbols, perhaps knowing that there is a multifaceted life that goes on underneath that cannot be slipped on as easily as Mohanbhai's shirt. But although we cannot dress ourselves in another person's culture and expect to know it, we can take steps in that direction. Ruth Benedict says more in *Patterns of Culture*:

> The truth of the matter is rather that the possible human institutions and motives are legion, on every plane of cultural simplicity or complexity, and that wisdom con-

sists in a greatly increased tolerance toward their divergencies. No man can thoroughly participate in any culture unless he has been brought up and has lived according to its forms but he can grant to other cultures the same significance to their participants which he recognizes in his own.[15]

Group Process

In the first group of eight students there were five women and three men and it was my first time with the program. The second group of four—two men and two women—had the benefit of my previous experience. In both groups orientation was a time of initial bonding; the students came with an openness and apparent nonjudgmental attitude. As time wore on, however, tensions did grow; friendships developed that were at once inclusive and exclusive, causing some hurt feelings. On entry into India the students encountered a totally different reality, with all familiar supports gone. Close friends, lovers, family, routines, space, landmarks, ways, faces—all were replaced with newness and unfamiliarity. They had to develop new ways of coping without alcohol, movies, TV, radio, drugs, discos, rock music, coffeehouses, bars, cars— none of these were available. They had only each other, their Indian companions, me, the village, and the countryside to help them cope. They had come on a trip with, for the most part, people whom they would not have chosen as their friends.

Although the students had left their competitive academic settings behind, there was still a sense of rivalry over who was learning Gujarati more quickly; who was most able to master the art of spinning by hand; who could connect with Indians; who fell sick and who remained healthy; who received mail and who didn't; who was better liked by our immediate circle; who was writing diligently in his/her journal; who managed to crank out letters encapsulating this complex array of stimuli; who could answer questions about America most accurately; who was having a rough time with the food, with the lack of toilet paper, with the mosquitoes, the heat, and the many strangers; who had ideas for his/her Independent Study Project; and who seemed most self-directed and on top of everything. All of these were potential areas of self-doubt. Each student had his/her particular area of concern, of insecurity, and of hope. They felt the weight of being conscious of their own behavior as well as that of their classmates.

How did the group's self-image and behavior affect the way Indians perceived them? Indians were often surprised by the informal, friendly relationship that the students had with me, as it was very different from the formal relationship they had with their own professors. In India it is difficult for young men and women to share leisure time comfortably together. The Indian students closely watched the male-female relations in our group—how much students touched each other, how they teased, and whether there were any sexual relationships (there weren't). Indians generally responded to those Americans who were most immediately outgoing, though the shy men would be approached before the quieter women. Some American students felt uncomfortable with the public disagreements that we had in response to a controversial question from an audience, partially because we were so obviously indelicate with one another's opinions. Others felt it was beneficial to show that we were not of one mind, that the U.S. is a place of many viewpoints, that that is one of its strong points. All agreed, however, that we needn't be vicious in our arguments.

For me, as academic director, it was an ongoing question as to how much I ought to intercede in problems that came up. I was always available to individuals needing to talk out a problem and also available if two people wanted to discuss a difficulty together. I went back and forth on how much initiative to take, how much care to give, or how much to allow them the space to experience their feelings, wrestle with them, and act on them if they so chose. I often wondered how responsible I was for making their stay a comfortable one. Were these differences part of their learning? Didn't they need to find their own ways out of the dilemmas? Didn't they need to learn to come forward if something was bothering them rather than relying on me to break the ice? Some students were better able to do this than others and would bring up issues with the group. Others held back and lived with their discomfort.

Humor became one of the major forms of acknowledgment of a problem and functioned, at least in part, as a solution. L. Robert Kohls in his book *Survival Kit for Overseas Living* chooses a sense of humor as one of the three most important coping skills needed in cross-cultural experience.[16] Oberg also makes reference to humor as part of the third stage of culture shock, when an individual begins to get his/her bearings and find a meaningful way to relate to the culture. After some time the group began to share their frustrations out of necessity; it's harder to chuckle with just oneself—it's more enlightening and releasing to share the hard/ridiculous times with others who know just what one is talking about.

Overall, the students found allies in one another. At times they came to the group when they needed support or someone to listen while they expressed their frustrations, questions, and fears. The group became a standard against which to measure one's own progress in adaptation. It also was a buffer zone, a barrier, and a form of insulation from full-time contact with and immersion in Indian culture. The students became gradually less dependent on the group as they grew more confident in their abilities to meet the world on their own. By the end of our stay in Sadra the students were increasingly ready to venture out on their own and began to feel that having to function so frequently as a group was a burden.

There were points at which the students would complain about spending so much time in the group. They had breakfast, language instruction, prayer, spinning, lunch, field visits in the afternoons, and dinner together; and they all lived together in the same rooms. There was no shortage of "togetherness." None of them were accustomed to being in such close quarters so much of the time. As American college students they had lived in dorms, but many had also lived in their own apartments and had led very independent, cosmopolitan lives. This lifestyle in Sadra felt like a reversion to camp or elementary school. They often felt they were being treated as children.

They were undergoing an unexpected aspect of culture shock. They hadn't anticipated that the extensive "groupiness" would be a problem. Only gradually through the semester were they able to see that most Indians live their whole lives in a group, whether it be their immediate family, school, religious order, or military service. Single apartments are scarce. The American students were aching for freedom and privacy, a lifestyle that few countries in the world, let alone India, can afford.

The students developed their own styles of adventuring. Angela took it slow—participating in dinner discussions, writing frequently in her journal or letters, gradually taking walks on her own, then riding into Ahmedabad with Cindy, unchaperoned. Her movement, like Margaret's, Tania's, Ed's, and Eric's, was gradual and consistent, with fewer lunges and retreats. Geoff, Al, and Penny, on the other hand, plunged in and then climbed out when the water got too cold or over their heads. Although they were very popular, Indian students found them erratic and unpredictable. Susan, Robin, and Daniel each ventured out quite a bit, but were consistent. Somehow they managed to share their inner selves while in public. Their outward movement was fueled more by a genuine curiosity and compassion than by a self-conscious obligation to "mingle" or "interact." They were less bound by an image of what a

good cross-cultural learner does and were driven more by
their own pressing questions. The fact that they were in
touch with these questions and that they were verbal,
social, and comfortable with people helped them to meet
with others in a more genuine way than those students
whose questions were deeply buried and confused by
swarms of "shoulds" and "coulds."

Towards the end of our three weeks in Sadra I wrote
this letter describing some of the cultural growth that the
students had experienced:

> It's interesting to watch the waves of involvement and
> distaste that roll in and out. On arrival, naturally, the
> students were very excited by all the donkeys, camels,
> monkeys, pigs, goats, sheep, cows, water buffaloes, and
> dogs that they saw. They were charmed by the friendly
> "namastes" that greeted us at the gate, and delighted by
> the spicy, different Indian food. That was Week One.
> Week Two was still enjoyable, but they felt a bit less
> enthusiastic about the haranguing, dirty urchins yelling
> "namaste" at the gate and the somewhat greasy and
> monotonous food served in the hostel dining area. Now
> it is Week Three: they have just come back from a three-
> day stay in village homes. As per the Indian custom of
> "guest is God," the students have been "cha-ed" (tea-ed)
> and dined so thoroughly that they have come back with
> fevers and upset stomachs. One woman talked about
> feeling incredibly drained and overfilled at the same
> time.
>
> A subtle aspect of the village visit experience was the
> return home—the light jar of reentry after having tuned
> oneself to reading all the subtle signs that establish a
> culture and make it different from another. The return is
> the assessment, the digestion, and the communication of
> the experience with all the ensuing challenge of articulat-
> ing a multidimensional happening.
>
> Village life has been exposed. They have found both the
> warm sense of community and the suffocation for lack of

intellectual air. They have smelled the fresh, clean scent of plants and flowers as well as the depressing abundance of human feces along the roadside. They have found the richness of culture in daily routines of *puja* in temples, in the colorful dress of gypsies and Rabaris and in the ease with which people visit each other unannounced.

Everyone had expected to have culture shock; they had expected to feel dashed and shattered by what they saw. But culture shock has a way of creeping in the back door, weaving its way into consciousness, more as an awareness of what is *not* there than of what is. Just as the Advaita Vedanta Master, Sri Nisargadatta Maharaj, says, "To know who you are, you must first investigate and know what you are not."[17]

Like barnacles, moving out and coming in, the students tested the cultural waters, each time changing just a little bit. They were testing their own capacities to absorb strangeness and to live in the unknown, discovering the edges of their tolerance and the boundaries of their own self-definition. They rejected that which was too threatening or too opposed to their own values; yet they were always a bit disappointed in doing so, knowing that behind the rejection was a further wealth of learning and new fields for exploration, knowing the rejection to be a resting place for a while before they opened themselves up again and reached out.

2

SINKING IN

Ahmedabad

The next four weeks based in Ahmedabad proved to be one of the most difficult portions of the semester, when the students finally experienced the hardships that are associated with the more severe stages of culture shock. During this time the students most acutely felt the tension between group responsibility and individual autonomy. In fact they experienced a range of apparent polarities—outside authority versus inner direction, exploring versus hiding, complaining versus learning, passivity versus activity. For most of this time, which included lectures, institutional visits, field trips to tribal areas and to a nearby agricultural university, the students had little control over their program. Lectures and field visits were all predetermined by the Vidyapith and me. I had taken suggestions from previous academic directors and the students, and I needed to be responsible to our program curriculum. This was the most structured time and the most stressful for many—often because of the lack of individual control over the schedule.

As a result of this difficulty, students began to explore the question of where control originates. They began to understand Aldous Huxley's statement, "Experience is not

51

what happens to you, it's what you do with what happens to you."[1] Or as Anne Janeway says, "While we are not responsible necessarily for the existence of a particular circumstance or event, we are responsible for its effect on us."[2] The more the students understood this concept, the more they learned about themselves—their cultural assumptions, beliefs, values—and the more they learned about India. Easier said than done. It is one thing to say that we have responsibility for our own experience and another to act with that consciousness. This "sinking in" period was a particularly good practice time.

All was not difficult, however. The students began to develop flexibility, spontaneity, and tolerance for ambiguity. They began to use the little available free time to explore, to adventure, and to have their own cross-cultural encounters.

Until ten years ago, Ahmedabad was the capital of Gujarat. It is a city of about three million, including Hindus (the majority) as well as Muslims, Jains, Sikhs, Jews, and Christians. As with all Indian cities, it is crowded and busy. There is a huge marketplace, a railroad station, bus stands, mosques, temples, and housing built during the sixteenth and seventeenth centuries in intricate mazes as protection against invasions. Although Ahmedabad's textile industry is declining, a growing chemical and electronics business contributes to making Gujarat the second most prosperous state in India. Gujarat was the state where Mohandas K. Gandhi was born, and Ahmedabad was the home of his first ashram in India.

The Gujarat Vidyapith was originally built in the countryside on the west bank of the Sabamathi River. Since the Vidyapith's inception in 1920, however, the city has expanded from the east side of the river to the west, so the university is now surrounded by wealthy cooperative housing societies and a business district. What was once a rural agricultural school has had to adjust to the new urban surroundings, physically and psychologically. The campus covers about one square city block and is enclosed by a wall. It houses students working for their master's degrees in education, social work, history, Gujarati, Hindi, economics, philosophy, and peace studies.

The American students and I lived in a self-contained hostel with bedroom doors opening out into a courtyard, which was often strung with our drying clothes. On arrival the students were delighted with the accommodations: there were two or three students to each room, which contained chairs and desks, rugs on the concrete floors, space, light, and a modicum of privacy. We took a tour of the campus, visiting the fairly extensive library, the dairy, the tribal museum, the publishing building, the spinning and prayer hall, the bank, the post office, and the khadi shop, which sold goods made by small village industries. Most importantly, the city was right there. At last the students were away from the boredom of rural life and could enjoy culture, excitement, a wider variety of people, museums, shops, and institutions. Most of the students were overjoyed to be in an urban atmosphere. Again, their expectations had kicked into gear—they associated their stay in the city with freedom, independence, and adventure.

Our schedule in Ahmedabad included four weeks of the Life and Culture Seminar, which consisted of lectures and field visits. One of the field visits was a five-day trip to the homes of the indigenous people of Gujarat, the tribal people who live in the hills on the borders of Gujarat and the adjacent states of Rajasthan, Madhya Pradesh and Maharashtra. We also took a trip to Anand, an agricultural university, and AMUL dairy, the largest cooperative dairy in Southeast Asia. Finally, there was the trip to the homes of Sadra students in the western part of Gujarat, called Saurashtra and known for its good food, embroidery, and hospitality. Between these trips there was a series of lectures by Vidyapith staff, professors from other universities, and directors of local institutions.

Although we were expected to continue daily spinning, our new schedule often made it difficult. At the same
time I continued to teach the Methods and Techniques in
Field Study course, speaking on data collection, interviewing, and contact development—to prepare students for
embarking on their Independent Study Projects.

A typical day started with breakfast at 7:30 at the
ladies' hostel, followed by one or two lectures; then spinning at 11:00, lunch at 12:00, and rest for two hours (especially necessary in the spring semester, when the tempera-
ture rose to one hundred degrees daily). In the afternoons
we visited museums, battered-women's homes, health
centers, dance academies, and economic research insti-
tutes. We returned in time for dinner with the women at the
ladies' hostel at 6:30, then had the evening free. Saturdays
were meant to be free, but because of our visits out of town
and the written assignments that were part of the Life and
Culture Seminar, the students seldom had a full day off.

Our day-to-day contact with Indians was of a very
different quality than in Sadra, which the students rapidly
began to miss, much to their surprise. We had primary
contact with two faculty members. One was responsible
for making academic arrangements; the other took care of
logistics and accompanied us on our trips out of Ahmedabad. They and the young man hired to aid us in the hostel
(make tea, boil water, buy snacks) were the Indians with
whom we had the most consistent contact. Although we
ate supper with a large group of women, communication
was minimal due to our very limited skill with Gujarati,
their lack of English, the noise, and the American students'
withdrawal as they imagined themselves to be the objects
of ridicule. We grew to miss the friendships that we had
built with Motobhai, his family, the staff, and students at
the rural campus. A sense of isolation set in, along with a
recognition that Sadra represented home for us, a place to
which we could return and receive a familylike welcome.

The erosion of the students' morale was due in part to this sense of isolation and to disappointment in the lectures. The students were accustomed to the American style of teaching. In India the teacher is the authority, has the final word, is the all-knower, leader and director of the learning experience. The student's role is to watch, listen, and receive—to be an empty vessel to be filled. Although questions were welcomed, the professors expected questions of clarification rather than the challenges they sometimes received from the Americans. The students in turn sometimes felt that the professor was evading their questions when he answered by delving into the history of the topic to more fully explain what he had said. These professors were likely to see a question as an opportunity and invitation to launch into a new sea of information and would seldom give a one-sentence answer.

The lectures were often dry and on subjects that held little fascination for the students. A particularly frustrating topic was religion. In an attempt to summarize and condense the essence of a religion, the lecturer might sound absolutist, simplistic, and contradictory; Hindu philosophy, Buddhism, and Jainism are extremely complex, with many paradoxical elements, which, when summarized, can sound quite confusing.

Some students managed to adjust and learn despite the difficulties. Eric wrote:

> Even if some of the lectures weren't valuable for me information-wise, I gained something by viewing them as how Indians think and express themselves on various issues. By adopting this approach, I got a lot more out of the material than I would have otherwise.

Or as Margaret said:

> Learning about Indian methods of teaching can be as interesting/enlightening as the information we were supposed to learn.

Another reason for the collapse of the students' morale was the unpredictable nature of the program. Although our days were tightly scheduled, it was not unusual for a plan to fall through—a lecturer to be absent or an institution to be closed. There were times when we were all set to go at eight o'clock but no one would come to get us. The students were always under pressure to be on time, and yet they would have to deal with buses, people, and events that were not. After three weeks the students grew very frustrated with having to live on tight schedules themselves while the rest of India didn't.

An interesting interplay developed between spontaneity and Vidyapith plans, between taking advantage of the extra time for independent exploration and feeling disappointed when a scheduled event didn't happen, between creatively responding to twists of fate and respecting the Vidyapith's responsibility for us. For example, we were once asked to rise at 5:30 A.M. to catch a train to a rural Gandhian girls' school, only to sit and "rest" upon arrival (we were not tired) and see a paltry one-room exhibit of a few items handcrafted by the students. Americans like to know what is going to happen next, what the sequence of events will be; we like to understand the logic. In a constant state of "not knowing," the students (and I) were naturally very uncomfortable. In this case we didn't really know where we were going or why. We had already seen a number of schools and this one seemed about the same as the others; no one spoke with us about the school, and there were no plans on arrival except to rest. The logic behind the Vidyapith's planning was obscure to us, and the students felt they had been hurried along to something that held little interest for them.

At first they were angry—which developed into a deadening passivity. Some students, however, took the time as an opportunity to explore. In the process they discovered a seventy-year-old Spanish missionary who had been working in the village for twenty years. They made their way to the village, where they found a large, ornate temple and a few disciples who were more than willing to talk to them. These contacts later became resource people during one student's Independent Study Project. These were times of creative exploration; they were ultimately the ground for the most fruitful learning experiences.

An excellent example of having to make the most out of an "interruption" was coping with the increasing riots, strikes, and disruptions that had begun to develop throughout Gujarat. In the spring we arrived in India just prior to state elections. The incumbent chief minister had issued a resolution to raise the number of reserved places for tribal and low-caste people in colleges and in the government—something similar to our affirmative action laws. The resolution was designed to attract votes, but in the long run it sparked fiery emotions from all castes, causing protests, strikes, bus burnings, and eventually major chaos throughout the whole state of Gujarat.

One of the results of these disturbances was a curfew in the city of Ahmedabad; also many institutions that we were to visit closed down. The challenge to us was to see this situation not as a blow to our program but as an opportunity to learn as much as possible about Ahmedabad, Gujarat, and India. We interviewed a wide variety of people about their opinions and feelings. An informal conversation at tea after a lecture became a debate among three colleagues who had very strong, differing opinions about the situation. It was fascinating to listen and watch how these three men expressed themselves to one another, knowing that although they disagreed intensely, they still liked each other and had to continue to work together.

The political state of affairs colored all our actions and discussions throughout the whole spring semester. And parallel to this, in the fall, Indira Gandhi's assassination affected the students' explorations and Independent Study

Projects. As Paul Rabinow says in his book *Reflections on Fieldwork in Morocco:*

> Interruptions and eruptions mock the field worker and his inquiry; more accurately, they may be said to inform his inquiry, to be an essential part of it. The constant breakdown, it seems to me, is not just an annoying accident but a core aspect of this type of inquiry.[3]

It was this lesson—to expect the unexpected, go with the flow, seize unexpected free time, make the most out of an apparently bad situation, let go of tightly held expectations, and discover what else was happening—that became the theater for growth. It was the gestalt of experiential learning. Once the students were able to get beyond the initial anger of being disappointed or misled (as they perceived it), they began to keep their eyes and ears open for possible adventures and opportunities that they could then initiate.

The students' self-initiated sojourning, as healthy and beneficial as it was to them, was often problematic to the Vidyapith staff. They had their own rules and regulations to uphold, based on extremely important premises. Although they were attempting to be as accommodating as possible to the Americans, they also had inherently different ideas on how decisions were made, who made them, and who obeyed them. In their organization, decisions were made by the vice-chancellor, and all problems, questions, and concerns had to first go through him or his assigned right-hand man. I, on the other hand, was attempting to be true to my philosophy of education, which entails a healthy dose of student participation. I felt that it was important for the students to have some say about where we were going and what we might see. As Edward Stewart says:

> From the earliest age, the American child is encouraged to decide for himself—to make up his own mind; he is encouraged to believe he himself is the best judge of what

he wants and what he should do. Even in those instances where the American cannot decide for himself, he still prizes the illusion that he is the locus of decision-making.... An American believes, ideally, that he should be his own source of information and opinions and, also, solve his own problems. The American usually expects to be able to express his opinions and to exert a fair influence in the final decision.[4]

The Vidyapith understood this to some extent, but it had little patience with the lengthy and wrangling discussions that sometimes ensued. Each group (the students and the Vidyapith) wanted to be consulted in decisions. The Vidyapith knew the language, the contacts, and the logistics of transportation. It was our host and felt responsible for our safety and well-being during our stay in Gujarat. It saw the Life and Culture Seminar as a time of exposure and felt responsible for introducing the students to a balanced view of Indian culture so that during the independent study period the students could go off by themselves and follow whatever leads they had been able to gather. But not until that point. The Vidyapith felt nervous when students acted on their own, worried that the students did not always have enough information to make wise choices. Independent movement while participating in a group is not part of Indian tradition. In contrast the students felt they had come to India to learn and should have more say in the program. After all, they were the students; the program was for them.

An incident on one of our field visits illustrates the tension. During our trip to the tribal area, the students met an elderly Gandhian named Shantibhai whom they promised to meet again in another two weeks in his home town of Anand, which we were scheduled to visit. The students wrote him a letter, informing him of the day and place of arrival. He met us and accompanied us on our dutiful rounds to the cow insemination farm, poultry plant, grain storehouse, and health-care center. At the end of the day

Shantibhai offered to introduce us to a 103-year-old woman who had worked with Gandhi. We left our Vidyapith chaperon with his friends and accompanied Shantibhai to visit this somewhat deaf but lucid lady. Shantibhai had other plans for us as well; here was a van and driver at his disposal and a pack of Americans he could show around. Not telling us his plans, he led us to his hostel in a boys' school, gave us a tour, drove by some relatives' house for a hello and goodby, and finally took us to an adjoining town, the birthplace of a famous independence leader, Sadar Patel.

We knew it was way past the agreed-upon time of return, but here was a sudden opportunity to go on an unplanned miniadventure with a friend that the students had made, rather than being accompanied by a Vidyapith bureaucrat. It was hard to resist. Although we had no idea where we were going, and although we knew we had to return by a certain time—a fact our friend, Shantibhai, was well aware of—we sat back and enjoyed the spontaneous tour, glad to be away from our dominating Vidyapith guide. On our return, the guide was extremely angry with our impromptu visits. He was not one to indulge in spontaneity himself and was not appreciative of our excursion, regardless of what we had learned.

Personalities aside, the incident proved to be a true cross-cultural lesson. The Vidyapith's responsibility to us was to arrange lectures and field visits. It also had to account for our whereabouts to the police at all times, part of the regulations concerning foreigners. The one day we chose to go with Shantibhai and be spontaneous was the same day that Indian students had called an all-day strike throughout Anand. Gujarat as a whole was going through a five-month period of disturbances, rioting, and protest; thus the Gujarat Vidyapith was legitimately concerned for our safety, which was its responsibility. As Americans, we were inexperienced in such situations and were somewhat oblivious to the potential danger.

The Vidyapith chaperon was also angry that we had blithely used the vehicle and driver, both of which were not the Vidyapith's and which had to be paid for. The dynamics were complex: we felt this particular guide had cried "wolf" too frequently, and he had exercised control for the sake of controlling too often, and yet as long as we were a group officially under the G.V. auspices, we had to abide by its rules. We could not exercise our individual will without first consulting our hosts—which had all too often resulted in a disguised and flowery no, or in great resistance.

Again and again we experienced this tension between our responsibility to the G.V. and the students' individual interests. They did learn to understand these dynamics and could even begin to get beyond the rigid personality of our guide to see his control as an overzealous performance of his duty.

With all of these frustrations the students became more passive and passive-aggressive. I found myself making nagging-mother statements: Please don't lie down when a principal of a school is talking to us. Come on time to lectures, even if you aren't thrilled. Keep up with the group—our guide will be offended if we all straggle behind. Pay attention when someone is talking to us, dress a little better, wash your clothes. You are an embarrassment to the rest of us and our hosts. Let me know if you'll be around for a meal—we need to let the kitchen know how much to make. You need to come to this Lions Club meeting because it is important to one of the people with whom we've had the most contact. I know none of you like him and feel that he is just using you for his own status, but he has also done a lot for us and we owe it to him. And so on.

The students were used to doing what they wanted, when they wanted. They were accustomed to showing respect when they felt someone deserved it, not when "duty" (a foreign concept, for sure) required it. The students had had little responsibility for the four-week program, being told when, where, and how to go and what to see. Yes, they had had some input but not in any ultimately satisfying way. At one point we had a "blame and complain" session designed to air feelings and frustrations, to identify who was responsible, and to recognize what they had learned up to this point. Their complaints verbatim:

> We're being led around as though on a leash, and in some instances being treated as an uneducated, helpless child.

> This program gives a one-sided view to another country—i.e., the rural development side. We need more focus on the arts. Most of the time I've been bored shitless, probably because almost all the time we are sitting in a chair listening to a person lecture us.

> I want to participate in more exciting aspects of India, like a tribal shaman. I am very disappointed we have not gotten some sort of yoga aspect in our daily activities.

> Because of the uncertainty of the schedule, it has been hard to schedule independent time more effectively.

> I wish I could be a more open person; slowly I open up. I wish I could do it faster.

> We need much more in the cultural area! If I were to go home right now, I couldn't honestly say I've "seen" India.

> Do more of what we want, be more part of decision making.

> Lack of freedom and individuality is a major problem. The sponsoring United States institution never stressed group activities, which misled me as to the content of this program.

We Americans undoubtedly value freedom of choice, autonomy, and independent decision making. As the five authors of *Habits of the Heart* have written:

> Freedom is perhaps the most resonant, deeply held American value.... Yet freedom turns out to mean being left alone by others, not having other people's values,

ideas, or styles of life forced on one, being free of arbitrary authority in work, family, or political life.... And yet if the entire world is made up of individuals, each endowed with the right to be free of others' demands, it becomes hard to forge bonds of attachment to, or cooperate with, other people since such bonds would imply obligations that necessarily impinge on one's freedom.[5]

Exactly our dilemma. And more. The students were in their late teens and early twenties. They were getting out, seeing the world on their own, testing their abilities to cope individually, sorting through a myriad of choices, developing intimate relationships, and searching for identities; independence was of the utmost importance. They were being constrained in ways that fundamentally challenged their psychological work-at-hand. They had the task of sorting out who was responsible for this clash that was impeding their developmental progress. Who was to blame? Was it the Gujarat Vidyapith with its responsibility for our safety, its own set of ideas of how group learning should be conducted, its belief that youth should show respect and obedience to their teachers, elders, and institutions? Was our American school to blame? Should it have chosen a different university in India? Should it have told the Vidyapith what to do? Or were the students to blame? Should they have been more accommodating, more ready to learn from everything they saw? Should they have waited patiently until their Independent Study Projects and, in the meantime, taken another look at their expectations of what India would be like? Whose program was this—the Gujarat Vidyapith's, the American school's, the students'?

The students (and I) were caught in a maze of a number of belief systems superimposed on one another. We were in an American experiential education program that chose to be associated with the G.V., which was hierarchical and group-oriented. On one level, we were learning about the society by agreeing to participate. On another level, though this was definitely experiential education, we were experiencing the Vidyapith itself, which was counter to what the students were most hungry for—determination of their own paths. They had chosen to participate in the program, but it wasn't what they had expected. Each had come with an idea of what India would be like—shamans, sitars, beggars, ornate temples adorned with erotic carvings, palm trees, beaches. All true, all there, but....

We had come to Gujarat, one of the areas least visited by tourists; we were seeing India as it was, the unromanticized version. At the Vidyapith we were witnessing the aging of an historical era that Gandhi had spearheaded. We were experiencing life as many Indian students do, only we didn't have their cultural viewpoints. And then culture shock had snuck up behind the students, catching them unawares. It was hard to be here, but for different reasons than had been anticipated. It wasn't the poverty, shacks, and starving children so much as it was the lack of control, the group format, the singleminded focus on rural development.

The students had been learning, but not what they had expected. They had been learning about another side of India, about themselves, about how to sustain themselves in barren times. They had learned about the United States, both by describing it and listening to Indians' thoughts and concerns, and by reflecting on the differences they had encountered thus far. Ed wrote:

> Learning has ranged from new knowledge about myself to knowledge of a society that I had never experienced. I have the ability to recognize my shortcomings to a greater degree, I have become infinitely more accepting of other people, and I have learned how to express myself, both intellectually and emotionally, to a greater degree. The idea of brotherhood among all men has become realistic in my mind. I am also seeing the U.S. from a new perspective, which has enlightened me as to the advantages and disadvantages of American culture.

Tania commented:

> I have definitely learned quite a lot about myself in the
> past month. I have learned to tap an inner strength, a
> spiritual aspect to myself, that before had not had the
> opportunity to surface. Spirituality is a subject that I have
> avoided before because it's one of those "deep, strange"
> subjects that one does not want to subject one's intellect
> to. I learned that spirituality and intellect have a working
> relationship and need not be an unapproachable subject.
> I have learned that I can rely on myself for my security,
> not on whatever cultural identities I may possess. It
> wasn't easy, and at times I really felt lost and, of course,
> I still have a lot to learn. I also have a new-found apprecia-
> tion for the good in my life, and a realization that the good
> in my life is constant and the bad is an illusion.

This was new for Tania; she was the local activist, who
had come to India with no particular interest in exploring
the spiritual world. She found that because of the lack of
close friends and family, she had to look to herself for her
major sustenance. She began to realize that her awareness
of an inner core helped her in her work rather than de-
tracted from it. Penny had felt at first patient and then
increasingly exasperated with the interminable visits to
rural development schemes. Despite this she had connected well with people:

> I've learned a great deal about friendships and hospital-
> ity. It is something I will try to bring back to New York. The
> people here have been so helpful. It really has made me
> reevaluate my own behavior in the U.S.A.

Daniel also talked about his inner development. He
had come from a difficult year in the States, had begun to
feel balanced, and then on coming to India had felt numb
and off balance:

> I have learned how dependent I am on external stimuli for

growth ... subsequently I have scoured my own heart for
some solid base which is independent of external stimuli.... I have gone though the same bitches about life that
I used to blame on "society," e.g., loss of direction, loss of
goals—but here, where there's no family, school, etc. to
blame, I see more clearly the side of my personality that
is responsible for my experience. I have learned that my
spiritual quest, the burning I have for "something more
than this way of life" must necessarily lead me through a
period of social responsibility. The spiritual goal, i.e., to
grow to a state of happiness and peace which is independent of all external actions, seems like a sensible goal
for me, in contrast to the worries of success, status, etc.,
that I left at Harvard. I learned a lot about American
society, i.e., pace of life, high standard of living, priorities.
I've learned that happiness and material goals are related
only insofar that you must be fed, clothed and sheltered
before you can be happy, but past that I'm doubtful ... I
learned, or relearned that the more love you put into an
endeavor, the richer that endeavor becomes.

Despite, and perhaps because of, the difficulties that
we had encountered thus far, the students began to find
ways to connect, to cope, and to take care of themselves.
They had begun to enter Gochenour and Janeway's fifth
and sixth stages in the process of cross-cultural awareness:

5. Develop conscious knowledge of oneself—as a
center, as a cultural being and one taking responsibility.

6. Consciously develop needed attributes and
skills—mental, emotional and physical.[6]

The students experienced a growing awareness of
themselves in India. They were gradually learning the skills
and attitudes necessary for traveling more deeply into the
culture and for understanding it more comprehensively.

Saurashtra

Although we had been heavily scheduled, the students had taken advantage of some of their free time to explore the city, find film stores, fabric shops, temples, ice cream parlors, book stalls, and restaurants. We had attended the *Ramlila*, a performance of an ancient Hindu story; two students had gone to a few lectures on Raja Yoga; others had started swimming at a nearby pool.

Towards the end of the Life and Culture Seminar there was a four-day break. We had been invited to visit the homes of Manubhai and Chunda, friends from Sadra.

First we went to Manubhai's house. To get there we took a six-hour bus ride, jostling along from 5:30 in the morning to 11:30. Then we switched buses, bumped along for another hour, and then disembarked at a barren crossroads with only a small tea stall. After a dusty two-mile walk, we reached Manubhai's village and were welcomed by his family. They offered tea, beds, and delicious, simple meals. They enjoyed and accepted our offers to help cook. Although the entire village soon came to view us (we were the first Westerners they had seen) and the courtyard was literally packed, we felt protected and welcomed.

It was *Divali*, the Hindu New Year. The next day we found a colorful chalk greeting to us, "Happy New Year Americans, Friends of the Heart." By five o'clock the courtyard was once again filled with people staring up at us in the loft where we slept. The day was rigorous; we must have had tea in fifteen different homes. We walked along the street, feeling like the Pied Piper of Hamelin, a parade of children following. As we entered each home, the wave of humanity would follow and once again surround us as we sat on the family's cots outside. At each place we sipped syrupy, sweet tea and sang a few songs. By the fifteenth house the students had become saturated with tea, attention, and fatigue; their final song selections were the theme songs from "Gilligan's Island" and "The Brady Bunch."

Our host gently ushered us home through the people-lined streets, fed us once again, but stepped back in respect to our protests against having any more. In the villages, most houses are lacking toilet facilities. Women generally go out to the fields in the dark, discreetly taking care of business in the early morning and late night. Men have the freedom of any time of day. We attempted to adapt ourselves to these rhythms, generating numerous jokes that lightened the awkward circumstances. We bathed in the field owned by Manubhai's family, using water from the well that watered their crops. Although there was a lot to adapt to—food, transportation (trucks, bullock carts, tractors, motorcycle-drawn carts), housing, living conditions, multitudes of staring people—it was a pleasure for us all, primarily because of our host's understanding and regard for our feelings and limitations.

Two days later we journeyed to Chundra's home. Even though we engaged in similar activities, the warmth was missing. This, in addition to the students' fatigue from being stared at constantly, made for a tense visit. In Chundra's home we were also treated as honored guests: we slept in the best beds, drank lots of tea, ate too much food, and toured the town. This time, however, we were showpieces, trophies that the Sadra student had brought home to enhance his status in the eyes of family, friends, and village. Once again we encountered questions about our material wealth, our connections, whether we could sponsor an Indian student in the United States. We had been asked these questions before but not in such a mercenary way.

Chundra took us around the village. Some people were genuinely curious, but others simply made us feel sucked dry, as though we were mainly providing our presence and our willingness to take photographs. As Margaret warned,

Be prepared to be stared at, followed around a lot and asked to sing at awkward moments. Try to get over feeling like an idiot in these situations as soon as possible—there's little you can do to avoid them. Be prepared to be stereotyped and seen generically as "An American/A Foreigner/A White Person/Somebody Different" instead of as yourself, complete with a complex and unique identity.

The two stays were quite a contrast, with the second one being more difficult because we were tired and because of Chundra's attitude. Once again the issue of control arose. In both homes each student saw it as his duty to anticipate and attend to our needs. But Manubhai also consulted us about how we would like to spend our time. He was sensitive to our need for protection from the constant curiosity. He interacted with us, giving and taking.

In the second home, where we expected mutual decision making and planning, we found that Chundra and his family felt it was their duty to plan and oversee our whole program. They believed they were relieving us of the burden of making any decisions or having any worries. And, at the same time, we felt like the property of our proud host, like baubles being passed from house to house.

We were indebted to both students for much of the arranging. We had had an opportunity to see remote villages. There was, however, an aspect of the experience which the students hadn't anticipated; we were also to be seen, studied, and experienced. We were two cultures peering at one another. Those haunting issues of wealth, opportunity, privilege, and white skin had all come up again.

After this short excursion into Saurashtra, everybody, including me, was ready for independence. They had had enough of group activities and felt more or less equipped to strike out on their own. The lectures had provided contacts for their projects. The field trips had yielded a sense of life beyond Vidyapith walls. Our numerous discussions together had helped the students sift through their experiences, and their own sojourns in and around the city had taught them how to go from here to there—precisely the next step.

3

INDEPENDENCE AND INTEGRATION

Vermont Preparation

> No man looks at the world with pristine eyes. He sees it
> edited by a definite set of customs and institutions and
> ways of thinking. Even in his philosophical probings he
> cannot go behind these stereotypes; his very concepts of
> the true and the false will still have reference to his
> particular traditional customs.[1]

So says Ruth Benedict in her book, *Patterns of Culture*.
The students had begun to explore this very important
concept during the orientation in Vermont. In their experience there they had begun to recognize themselves as
culturally shaped people coming from a certain set of
assumptions, expectations, and frames of reference.

One of the ways the students began their exploration
was through an exercise called simply "The Drop-Off,"
developed in the 1960s by Desmond M. Conner. The exercise
has a number of interrelated objectives. Originally, it was
designed to teach field study skills: how to learn about a
place by observing, interviewing, researching, participating,
and listening. It then became apparent that, through the

experience, people also became aware of their own learning process, and what they did and did not feel comfortable with. They not only learned from the information and data they gathered but also from what they didn't find, by thinking about whom they didn't approach and why, which areas they refrained from exploring and why. They began to learn from both the substance of and the gaps in their experience.

There are four basic components to the exercise: (1) preparation, (2) a community visit, (3) the compilation of anecdotes, and (4) systematic analysis. The experience consisted of dropping each student off in a small New England town within a thirty-mile radius of home base. They remained there for three to four hours; their task was to find out as much about that town as possible within the allotted time. They could talk with inhabitants, make maps, note the architecture and general layout of the town.[2]

One could feel the nervous tension in the big, old Ugly Duckling rent-a-car station wagon as we started off to do the exercise. Like the kindergartners I used to teach, the students finished off the bag lunches in the car before we reached the first town, where the first one got pushed out like a bird out of a nest. On we went until the group had dwindled to the last one. They would be picked up in turn in another three or four hours.

Some brought cameras, all took pen and pad, one took a tape recorder. The time passed quickly. I had lunch and did some preparation work for later in the week until it was time for the pick-up. They had had a myriad of experiences. Each person got in the car, bubbling with his/her adventures. A few students had started out by sitting on a bench in the center of town. Others went directly to the cemetery, others to a library or other source of information. A few struck up conversations right away. One of the decisions they had to make was how they would present themselves to people: were they students, or a relative from out of town, journalist, potential homeowner, or tourist?

Margaret entered a church, found a woman cleaning, and offered to help, not knowing how to best initiate and connect. The cleaning woman was bewildered by this stranger wanting to do a task that few do willingly in their own home. She was rather cold and uncommunicative. Margaret left and tried again elsewhere, this time approaching a woman at the post office. Margaret stated her mission: she was a student doing research on Westminster and wanted to know to whom she could talk. This approach worked better; the context and background made more sense to the postmistress. She directed Margaret to a ninety-year-old woman who had lived in town all her life. Margaret stayed with the old woman, had tea, and listened for at least an hour. She had learned something about approach, trust building, and productive ways to communicate her needs and interests.

Robin's question, once she had found her informant, was how much she should try to direct the conversation. She had found a "writer" in town who, in fact, drank perhaps too frequently and had not written much in the last few years. Should she keep the man on target, asking him to get back to her questions about the town, or should she not interfere, let him ramble on, build trust and follow his lead into areas that she might not have anticipated? This question would frequently arise again in India during their Independent Study Projects.

The students not only had to get information from a number of sources, but they also had to form hypotheses based on that information. For example, a student, having noticed the large number of children's gravestones dated 1886, would conclude that there might have been some sort of epidemic that year. Students were exposed to the process of *observation, interpretation,* and finally *evaluation* that stemmed from the seemingly random pieces of evidence. Then they needed to verify and double-check the information. They needed to do the same while speaking with people: to be willing to doubt their sources and to realize there may be as many truths as there are people involved. They became creative about where and how to pick up clues—for example, they spoke with children, read notices on the community bulletin board, looked at the most prominently displayed items in stores, and made interpretations based on the kinds of cars in town: pick-ups, four-wheel drives, foreign cars. They noticed who was on the street, who was not, how many churches there were and whether there were run-down areas, fancy inns, or newly built condominiums.

The drop-off exercise proved to be one of the most instructive activities done during the orientation. The students could readily see that a purely intellectual under-standing of the skills necessary for entering a foreign culture was inadequate; they had to start practicing the skills they already possessed and begin developing the ones that they lacked. They realized how much data could be collected in a relatively short amount of time if one is intent upon it. They came to know more about the United States by exploring a small rural town in New England and in the process were able to step back and look at their own communities.

Donald Batchelder has some wisdom to offer on this point:

> We tend to define the center as that special place where we are known, where we know others, where things mean much to us, and where we ourselves have both identity and meaning, family, school, town and local region ... every place has special meaning for people in it; every place represents the center of the world. The number of such centers is incalculable, and no one student or traveler can experience all of them, but once a conscious breakthrough to a second center is made, a life-long perspective and collection can begin.[3]

Throughout the semester in India, students would refer back to this first exercise, using it as proof that they could do the unexpected. Tania, Angela, Eric, and Margaret all remarked that they had never interviewed people before, never approached strangers to ask questions of any depth. They were surprised at their own capacities. Angela wrote:

> My learning during the Vermont drop-off was that I can question people—strangers—and learn about personal life and feelings. It gave me a tremendous feeling of accomplishment; I can still look back on it with pride as an example of a time when I tried something scary and new and succeeded.

This laid a foundation of self-confidence. If they could face one challenge, feel the tension but go on through and come successfully out the other side, they would be able to transfer that lesson and apply it in India.

Projects

The Independent Study Project (ISP) was, finally, the time when the students could arrange their own schedules and make their own decisions about whom they would see, when, and what they would ask. The students had been preparing for their ISPs since they applied to the program. The language study, the Life and Culture Seminar (LCS), and the Methods and Techniques of Field Study (MTFS) were all part of building a foundation from which to explore their environment. Language ideally supplied a means of communication, LCS provided information and contacts, and MTFS equipped the students with tools to interview, collect, analyze, and organize data. By the time the ISPs rolled around, the students had written three proposals outlining their questions, methodologies, and plans of action.

This particular part of the program was both a high point and a cause for anxiety. There were three weeks with

no other responsibilities but to their own project. They
looked forward to finally being able to follow the dictates of
their hearts, to test themselves alone in Indian society. The
anxiety came from being unclear as to what those inner
dictates were. They felt they risked making the "wrong
decision," fearing that they would not get the most out of
the experience. They had fears of not "doing well," stemming from past academic experience. They all wanted to
say something new, to make a contribution to their field.
Some were afraid of being out on their own, of not finding
housing, of being a guest all the time in someone's home. All
the pressure we felt as a group before was coming to bear
on them individually. Some chose to be away from the
hostel in Ahmedabad for almost the entire time; most
others came and went, going out for a few days, then
returning to regather themselves. A very few stayed the
whole time since their studies were located in Ahmedabad.

Once again the process was different for each student.
Some came with clear ideas about their topic. Margaret
wanted to stay in a convent to "add a little concrete
physical reality to all the textbook philosophies I had been
studying through the rose-colored glasses of intellectual-
ism." Susan wanted to dance, and Al wanted to study with
a man he had heard about who had magical powers and
could track wild tigers at night. Though they were encouraged to remain flexible, they held with their choices.

Daniel and Tania knew they were interested in particular areas—spirituality and rural development, respec-
tively—but they had no idea what form their exploration
would take. Penny, Cindy, Ed, and Robin had no idea what
they wanted to do, or, rather, they had so many ideas they
didn't know which one to choose. Their task was the most
difficult; they had to figure out what held the greatest
interest for them, decide which project was particularly
unique to being in India, and settle on one that hit the
deepest on the most levels. It has been said that within

every question lies the answer. The key to coming up with a satisfying project was asking questions of oneself and of others. Those who were pushed by some craving from inside to understand, to grasp, and to clarify were the ones who had the most successful projects. As Gordon Murray says in *Beyond Experience*, "Successful projects integrate the past with the present, the home culture with the new culture, the head with the heart, the demands of academe with 'where you're at.' "[4]

Robin's was a successful project according to the above definition. After considering at least five other possible topics, Robin eventually settled on one that combined aspects of all her previous interests.

During orientation in the United States Robin had shared her reasons for wanting to go to India. She intended eventually to join the Peace Corps so she hoped this trip would be a good test of her coping abilities. At this point, she was not clear on her career choices, and she approached her ISP with a number of options—perhaps she could study the caste system in Sadra, or an untouchable housing development program. No, that wasn't exactly what she wanted. Maybe she could travel with gypsies as they wandered from job to job, herding their donkeys along the way. That was not very feasible. Perhaps she could go to Mt. Abu to study universal peace and meditation with the Raja Yoga sect; she had attended a few lectures in Ahmedabad, but this option didn't quite fit either.

Aha! Perhaps she could work with a health-care organization in Anand that helped malnourished mothers and their newborn. This idea rang true much more strongly than the others. Unfortunately, the agency couldn't logistically manage her stay. So, striking out with the same focus, she tried a local group in Ahmedabad, but after waiting in their office for one and a half hours without hearing a word, she stalked out. Finally, still holding on to her interest in women and children's health care, she took a bus out to a nearby village and tracked down a woman doctor to whom she had been referred. At last she had found the perfect situation. She lived with the doctor next to the hospital and volunteered daily at the nearby Primary Health Care Center (PHCC)—the government-managed, village medical facility.

While at the PHCC, she made home visits, carried out a small survey in two villages, attended two births, and conferred with her friend, Dr. Joshi, asking her questions continuously. All through the semester Robin had felt free to ask anyone about anything that popped into her mind. Her genuine nonjudgmental curiosity made people feel comfortable in answering honestly. Her willingness to ask "dumb questions," her unabashed roaming from one topic to another were indicative of an openness and flexibility that enabled her to wait until she found the best ISP situation for herself. She didn't spend much time worrying about what others would think.

Geoff went through a very different process, with a different outcome. He had come to India wanting to immerse himself in a community of people that lived in a remote area, far away from Western life as he knew it in Southern California. He, however, found a project that interested him after only two weeks of being in Sadra. He was reading the Sunday paper when he came across an article about a huge dam being built in Gujarat that was to be funded by the World Bank. Apparently, there was debate about whether the two million displaced people— primarily tribal—were getting the promised compensation. Geoff decided to make a study of the dam and the controversies surrounding its construction.

Geoff was gone from the hostel for the duration of the three weeks. He went first to Surat to a study center where he found a few helpful specialists. He then managed to find the correct buses to go to the once-grand town of Rajpipla, in its heyday a settlement for Parsis and Maharajas. He found housing with a Parsi woman who gathered him to her bosom as a mother takes a son. He interviewed officials, hearing views from all sides, saw the dam site, and visited some of the evacuated villages. He thus did extensive research using both books and human resources. This intellectual mode was attractive to the English major in him; the project appealed to his journalist/debater experience, but he found that after all that effort, all the muckraking and skulking around, he wished he had gone with his first choice, his "heart's desire" as he described it.

He wished he could have countered the voice inside that had coached him to take the familiar, intellectual approach; he did make it out to a remote area but he hadn't sunk himself in there. He had learned a tremendous amount about traveling and trusting people. He had learned to enjoy making his own way, but in the end he said:

> I am sorry I didn't go with my heart in respect to topic selection. Although I derived a great deal from the project overall, I would still have gotten more from being a fisherman or shepherd as I initially thought. *Shun karun?* What to do?

Daniel, Eric, and Penny worked on projects that helped define aspects of themselves that were still a mix of feelings and impressions. Daniel took on the broad topic of religion and spirituality; Eric delved into the Jewish community and Judaism, a previously unexplored part of himself; and Penny listened and talked with women, in search of a better understanding of what that role has meant to her.

Eric decided early on to study the small Jewish community in Ahmedabad. He had come once before to India but only as a tourist. Now he had an opportunity to get to know the people of India more intimately, and to broaden his understanding of his own Jewish heritage by examining the manifestation of Judaism in Gujarat. He interviewed over twenty people, went to their homes and their workplaces, discovered the subtle hierarchies and the splits and conflicts within the community. He learned about Jewish ritual as it has been influenced by Indian culture, the history of Jews in India, and how these Jews felt about Israel and India (particularly interesting since India does not have diplomatic ties with Israel).

He developed cultural compatriots whom he hadn't known existed, people with totally different backgrounds but with shared traditions. He had traveled 12,000 miles to visit another culture only to find a variation of his own.

Much to her surprise, Penny found herself interested in the lives of Indian women. She decided to talk with some who were involved in a home for battered women. She interviewed the directors and stayed over three nights, sharing the room with a woman whom she also interviewed. Penny speaks well for herself:

> I think the hardest question I've put to myself these past three weeks is why I was interested in learning about women's problems. At first, I came up with only blanks. I was never overly involved with women's issues in the United States. I didn't know the history of the movement in my own country, why should I all of a sudden take an interest in it here? At home I didn't define myself as first a woman, then a family member, student, New Yorker and American. When I thought about my position in society, I never placed myself in various definitive categories. In fact, I never thought about my position in society. When I had a paper to complete I was a student, when I was having problems with my love life I was a woman, when there was a conflict in family relations I was a daughter, sister or niece. But there was never one overriding category in which I could place myself. I was just a person— a face in the crowd.

> But all that changed the moment I stepped off the plane in Bombay. I, all of a sudden, became conscious of myself being a woman—a modern, Westernized woman. I was conscious of the way I dressed; why was I disguising my femininity behind these shabby black sweat pants? I was conscious of the way I carried myself; I felt gawkish and

ten feet tall. I was conscious of the way I spoke: Why do I always use such vulgar language? Why am I so loud? It was as though a part of me had left my body and was reviewing and censoring all of my actions and my reactions to other people. I knew I was no longer just a face in the crowd, but I hadn't realized that the crowd would now be facing me. For the next three months I would have to prepare myself to be constantly scrutinized as a woman and as an American. I would become the stereotypes associated with the West.

My own identity, Penny, from New York, was now irrelevant. I was only Ila (Penny's Indian name), the American woman. Everything I once used to describe myself was now buried under the heading of "woman"—Western woman. I became overly sensitive to the position of women in Indian society primarily because I was now so aware of my own precarious situation. The word "woman" connotes an entirely different meaning in India; where did I stand within this new meaning? I suddenly felt myself as the representative of the Western connotation of the word, but I was in a country which places women in a less fortunate light. I was floundering somewhere in between the two. Representing one way of life, but living within another, raised many questions about womanhood in general. At first I felt as though there were no bonds linking Indian and American women. Ironically, I was now drawn to them and interested in their problems because I saw myself as a woman. Our differences drew us together.

To me this last sentence is the crux of cross-cultural learning. Penny, once freed from the role definitions given her by her own culture, became conscious of an aspect of herself, her womanhood, which had been redefined by coming to India. By studying Indian "women caught between the equality on paper and the actual persistent inequality," she learned that "these women are beginning to define themselves not in terms of an ideal or another

person, but in terms of their own needs and desires." This
was what Penny, herself, was sorting out. She went on to
say that "they are beginning to see that their personal
happiness should not be gauged in terms of pleasing another but in terms of self-fulfillment." She continues by
describing what she gained from being with these women:

> I learned that the women who use the facilities at both
> these institutions (a battered women's shelter and social
> service organization) are not "social rejects." Though
> introverted, they are not meek. They are incredibly strong.
> They are victims of an unfortunate situation, but rather
> than allowing the situation to get the better of them, they
> have stood up against their families. Though I sometimes
> still feel that "I have it better than them," I know I am not
> a better person because of it. I know I do not have their
> courage and strength. This is the most powerful thing I
> have learned about them and about myself.[5]

Ed, like Penny and Robin, had so many ideas of what
he wanted to do that he had a hard time settling on one
topic. He chose to spend a week at a Gandhian school for
tribal children a few hours north of Ahmedabad. This was
an interesting choice for Ed. He had come to India with a
keen interest in learning about Gandhi; he held high expectations of the people who worked in such institutions as the
Gandhian school. His weekend village visit back in Sadra
had been with one of the faculty members at the Vidyapith
rural campus. Ed had had a terrible time listening to the
man yell at his wife and children, watching him strip off his
khadi clothing and change into polyester bell-bottoms as
soon as he got home. Gandhian ideas meant nothing to him,
much to Ed's shock and disappointment.

During the Life and Culture Seminar we had met the
principal of Lokniketan, a primary and secondary school
based on Gandhian ideals located in the low-income district of Banaskantha. He had kindly taken us around to his
school, given us a tour of the dry northern plains, and

invited Ed to return and stay with him. Ed decided to accept his invitation to return and find out what kind of education the tribal children were really getting. Did the principal of this school have to hire non-Gandhians as the Vidyapith appeared to do? What could be done with so little money? How were Gandhi's values and ideals passed on?

Fortunately, Ed found a willing interpreter, who helped him ask questions during his brief stay. He came to understand the difficulty of attracting good, strong teachers out to small villages, with the promise of very little pay. The teachers were nice enough but they were not necessarily well qualified in their field or at all familiar with who Gandhi really was. Ed's project helped him understand better how the lack of resources can obstruct the manifestations of one's ideals.

Daniel had wanted to find a Holy Man:

> I came to India looking for that vague something. In particular I came to India searching for a sage, that funny old man with a light in his eyes.... In retrospect, the desire to find a religious guide or master was an articulation of a deeper rooted psychological search for what Carl Gustav Jung has called the Self.... It was only after two months that I managed to make a distinction, in my own mind, between the act of studying religions and searching for something religious.

His continuing search for that Self and a focus for his ISP went through many changes. First he thought about studying with Dixit Sahib, his friend with the chicken soup; then he thought of studying at the temple he had found during the deadly, passive trip to Anand. He became frustrated by all the outward signs of religion, which lacked the depth and spirit which he saw evident in folk dance and daily rural life. He eventually chose to make a pilgrimage:

> The idea of pilgrimage emerged in the same way as had my decision to travel to India—spontaneously and with

> hidden unconscious meaning ... by acting out the pilgrimage, I attempted to realize the content that was latent in my unconscious.

He found himself a guide and proceeded to journey to some of Gujarat's holy places. In his wanderings he encountered *Sannyasis* (usually men who have renounced the world, donned orange robes, and dedicated the rest of their lives to the worship of God), priests, and common people working on farms and in shops along the way. After three weeks:

> I became disillusioned with the Sannyasis, who did not necessarily seem any more enlightened than these warm and benevolent lay people. In other words, I have come to the conclusion that sincere spirituality brings one in close contact with the world, that the inward and outward realms are but part of the same continuum ... the pilgrimage was inward, completely inward, only to uncover springs that pushed me outward. Where to next, I do not know, but definitely on to a more thorough synthesis of the outer and inner worlds.

Tania had come to feel the need for synthesis as well, but her journey had started from the outward end of the spectrum. She came with a keen interest in rural development. She knew from the start that she wanted to study how social activists were working to change the society. She, of all the students, had benefited from the many lecturers and field trips concerned with social conditions. Although she wasn't clear how she would follow through, the clarity of her questions about poverty, housing, power structures, opportunity, exploitation, and acceptance all led her from one resource to another until she found an organization that seemed to combine and address her burning interests. Through her work with the Ahmedabad Study Action Group, a group dedicated to designing and building better low-income housing with tenant participation, she came to understand the scope of the questions she had been asking about poverty and its eradication. She developed a long-term perspective that acknowledged the complexity of the issues involved.

She encountered hopelessness, massive poverty, thirty-year-old programs that had made little dent in the overall problems. She found a verbally willing but lethargic government that ignored the statistics at hand. She discovered the world of corruption, self-interest, and exploitation, against which few protested. There were times during her ISP when she was in tears, feeling overwhelmed by the state of India, the world, and her own apparent insignificance. She was working, however, with a number of individuals who she considered models, people who had committed their skills to solving these problems and who had found ways to sustain themselves—to live a full life now while working towards a better future. She realized the essential need for inner sustenance. She found herself looking inward, reading more philosophical texts. She and Daniel had long talks on the importance of integrating the world outside with the world inside.

By the end of three weeks she had reconciled the disparity between these two worlds and was ready to make a lifelong commitment to the study of these problems.

> I have a better understanding of where my drive in this area comes from and how to apply it to the future. This paper is far from finished; I have developed a concrete base on which to build further knowledge and have gained a substantial understanding of the direction I am going and how my continuous studies will guide me. It is an introduction to the beginning of an interesting and fulfilling life.

The Independent Study Project had helped Tania focus on her life's work. She came away much clearer on what she wanted to do for the rest of her time at college and beyond.

Susan and Angela had both made strong academic choices in college. Their programs were set. Susan was a math and computer science major—very probably headed for a management position in a large company. Angela was a Medieval Europe scholar; she intended to apply for fellowships in England and France. By coming to India both students had decided to change direction, to explore other roads, sensing that these might give perspective to their previous choices.

In Susan's effort to leave academia behind, she chose to study Indian dance by learning it rather than by simply conducting interviews and analyzing it intellectually. She danced for three solid weeks, from 8:00 A.M. to 6:00 P.M. every day, learning the basic steps to *Kathakali* and *Bharat Natyam,* both of which require at least six years of training. Her written report consisted of an extremely detailed description of each day's lesson and reflection about the dynamics she saw around her:

> I was able to fully immerse myself in Indian classical dance during my Independent Study Project. Rather than watching dance and talking about dance and reading about dance, I actually danced myself. In this way I saw dance from the inside out, not the outside in, and was therefore able to learn not only physical movements and steps but a lot about the culture that produces such dance. The friendship I developed with my teacher and his family furthered my understanding of Indian life, culture and dance.

But she had learned that just engaging in the form of a culture is not enough to fully understand it:

> The feelings you need to express to portray Krishna or Ram or an Indian woman are not the sort of things you can learn quickly but are ideas that Indian children are brought up with from their earliest childhood. Acting like Krishna is not merely a physical thing but religious and spiritual as well.

Angela decided to study Gujarati poetry. With the help of Motobhai, the language teacher, she translated a lengthy poem by Mirabahen, our poet friend from Sadra. Even more important to her, she wrote a number of her own poems, expressing thoughts and impressions that she had absorbed throughout the semester. She met with four poets who were very impressed with both the translation and her original poems:

> My own poetry brought me many realizations and "ahas." To write it I had to take my feelings about India, my thoughts about Indian life and philosophy and analyze them so I could verbalize them. I had to isolate my own attitudes and understand what I wanted to say. This took me back to earlier experiences in India, my reasons for coming, my whole philosophy of life and Indian influence on it. It made a lot of things clearer. I also was delighted with the discovery that I can write good poetry—one of the most satisfying things I've learned.

Cindy, the anthropology major and resident juggler, had decided to research the very old tradition of Rajasthani puppetry—looking at its past, present, and future problems. She went to museums, talked to curators, artists, scholars, and government handicraft people. Most important for her, however, was the time she spent in the cramped hut of Govindji, a puppet carver and performer by caste. She spent long hours with him and his family, learning how to carve the puppets, communicating in a mix of Hindi and Gujarati, and learning a tremendous amount about his day-to-day life. At the end of the semester she wrote this about what she had learned:

> I learned that it must take a very long period of observation and interaction with a group of people in order to understand their social relationships and lifestyles. I went into Govindji's community expecting to *observe, take meaningful notes, and study their lives.* Well, I ended

up becoming too attached to the people to be so objective. I found that it's nearly impossible to generalize about the lifestyle of a group because a group is made up of individuals and each is different. I also realized the amount of time one would have to live with a group before they accepted your presence enough to resume their normal lives. I learned that my presence must also be taken into account as a factor in Govindji's family's behavior. Did they really drink so much tea every day or was Cindy, the Guest, a good excuse to do so?

Finally, the most important thing I realized is that it is nearly impossible to escape becoming attached to the people one studies. I learned that this affection can get in the way of objective observation, but the interaction itself provides another way of personal observation. Through writing up my ISP, I came to realize how much I had come to sympathize with the plight of traditional artists like Govindji.

The ISPs were not easy, however. The students now had to negotiate their way around by themselves. They had to make phone calls, catch buses, take rickshaws, find housing, make contacts who were willing to help them, and dive into the unknown. They were confronted, once again, with their expectations and images. Margaret had been very clear from the beginning of the program that she wanted to stay in a convent, that she wanted to immerse herself in Eastern philosophy—physically, emotionally, and, she hoped, spiritually. She had high expectations of herself academically and so felt pressured to perform as she had in the United States. Her project did not progress smoothly. Contacts fell through, schedules conflicted, but more importantly, she was horrified to find that after twenty-four hours of living the arduous life of a Jain nun she hated it! I'll let Margaret tell her story:

Ringed with my horde of dangerous and far-too-large expectations, I donned a white sari, kicked off my sandals, and waltzed out the hostel door minus all worldly possessions, including an outward identity, to "become a Jain nun" and simultaneously justify my existence. I took a vow, and for a very painful and enlightening twenty-four hours, I chanted mantras, went begging (barefoot), pulled out my hair, slept on the floor, and in general had a wretched time. When I was confronted with the opportunity to take another twenty-four-hour vow, I found myself recoiling in squeamish horror, stammering nonsense about a doctor's appointment I could not miss on Monday. I was released and I crawled home to watch my ISP disintegrate, along with an unhealthy store of self-respect.

I proceeded to spend a considerable amount of time struggling with my own "wimpishness" and mentally fussing and fuming at the Jain nuns, whom I had by then categorized as the epitome of misguided masochism, for so rudely pointing this wimpishness out to me. Should I go back and make myself voluntarily miserable for two and a half more weeks for the sole, selfish sake of proving to myself that "I could do it"? Or should I scrap the entire project, leaving my ego to rot, and then have to deal with my all-too-frequent guilt feelings about never finishing the things I start? I was bitterly disappointed in the whole situation, and most of all in myself.

After a morning of crying on Jennifer, staring stupidly out the window, and hiding between the earphones of my Walkman, I finally began to give myself a break, looking thoughtfully at some of the reasons behind my violent reaction to this "nunning experience" and trusting myself and my instincts enough to believe my reactions were honest and valid, not necessarily wimpy and bad. My ISP suddenly earthquaked its way into a new, more meaningful setting. A scornful condemnation of what the nuns did happily flipped into an intrigued and almost respectful curiosity as to why they did it. Surely there must be a very powerful core of sacred somethingness to lead a nun through a lifetime of world renunciation, pain, discipline, submission, and complete inanity.

Margaret then proceeded to go to an ashram, find an interpreter, interview nuns, and talk with other women who had not taken vows but who had dedicated their lives to studying Jainism. At the end of her ISP, Margaret had this to say:

> Now my interviews are complete, my frustrations and confusions about my nunning experience are more or less worked through, and my images of the nuns themselves have been healthily converted from "misguided masochists" to sincere and devout women who choose to express their spirituality in a very different way (that may not always make sense to those of us not allowed inside the inner sacred circle, but that should remain valid as worthy of respect nonetheless).... I conclude— with a certain amount of pride for having stuck it out this long—with a thoughtful respect for the different ways people can choose to express their devotion to God, and a deeper trust in my own religious instincts that will hopefully allow me to keep fine-tuning my definition of religion, discarding some of the romantic myths in favor of those realities that I can more easily sink a psychic anchor into.

As Margaret herself said, she had gone in with great expectations that soon were dashed. She picked herself up, looked at the root of those expectations, and began to probe again, this time with different questions, stemming from a dramatically different reality than she had expected.

Al, too, had started off with very high expectations. They also did not come to fruition, but he was not able to turn the situation around. He was less willing to give up his feelings of disappointment and move beyond them to see what was really happening. Al had gone down to a remote part of Gujarat, to the Dang tribal area; he had heard of a Gandhian worker, who, among other things, stalked wild tigers at night. He had first heard of this man during orientation in the United States; a previous group had met him and told us of his feats. Al was hooked on that idea and would consider nothing else. Unfortunately, when he arrived the man was busy, as was his friend, the eccentric anthropologist, who also knew his way around the tribal area. A local banker offered to take Al out on a one-day excursion but never seemed to get the time. Al spent his ISP behind earphones, reading a book in a hotel room, or warding off multitudes of curious village children when outside.

He had gone down expecting to be with this man or to find a shaman who could teach him his powerful ways. He could not comprehend the possibility that this might be a complicated task, taking far longer than three weeks. He had been disappointed. Not finding what he expected, he didn't know what to do. He couldn't see these disappointments as signposts directing him towards another route, and so he closed off possible paths by holding tight to his blinders. He came back and wrote a research paper based on library research and secondary resources. He had learned that the Dang were Westernized, Hinduized—they did not conform to the romantic image he had had in mind. The people in and around Alwha had become townspeople, but what happened beyond the town? He knew there was more but couldn't find a way to get out there. He was impatient with the slow work of building trust that is necessary to enter a remote, very different culture.

In the end, what did he learn? I don't know. I'm afraid he came away with only disappointment, both with the Dang people and with himself. Another rejection, another instance of miscommunication and proof of the lack of closeness in the world Al inhabited. He had traveled to Norway, to Italy, and now to India, hoping to touch and be touched and yet failing—why? Because, perhaps, of not being able to accept himself or others as they were. He craved more meaning in life. He devoured Carlos Castaneda books, read philosophy, loved talking about yogis and people with extraordinary powers but was unable to catch hold of any of that magic within himself.

Presentations

The students returned to the hostel after three weeks. They had four days to prepare for their hour-long presentation and to write a paper about their research. The atmosphere was tense, with people staying up all night, working to meet this deadline. The final day in Ahmedabad was very moving. The students invited their close friends and project advisors to the presentations. Susan, dressed in a sari, danced magnificently. Her teacher sat in front, beating out the teaching rhythm on wooden sticks. Cindy gave a summary of what she had learned about the history and present difficulties facing the caste of puppet makers with whom she had been an apprentice. Her teacher and his family came, bringing their puppets to demonstrate how they worked. And so it went on. Daniel read from parts of his paper. Angela read her poetry. Robin invited us to pretend we were health planners meeting together to decide on the best health-care policy. Geoff showed maps of the area to be affected by the dam. Margaret showed us her mask, dusting broom, and red begging bowl, all part of her "nunning" paraphernalia.

I was tremendously moved by the effort, determination, and openness with which most of the students approached their projects. Daniel had listened carefully to himself and taken himself seriously. He hadn't settled for an easy project but had continued to pay attention to what he needed, even though the rationale for his search for a holy man was amorphous and difficult to describe. Despite that difficulty, and with the pressure of Harvard's academic expectations in his mind, he kept hold of his questions and was willing to wrestle with his confusion. He took the risk of being labeled as "too subjective," "not scientific enough" and went ahead with his explorations, later on weaving his intellectual perspective into his paper.

Margaret had also held fast to the questions that propelled her, though they led her on a different route than she had anticipated. She had come with very high expectations, a whole mural of images in her head, that were washed out in less than twenty-four hours. She had gone way down, feeling angry, lost, and defeated, and then was able to snap back, pick up the pieces and see the totally different picture which had begun to replace the images that had been washed away. That had been very hard to do. Many blocks had been in her way, many disappointments. She ended up not enjoying her ISP but was proud that she had stuck with it and satisfied when she found that the nuns actually experienced the spiritual peeling away that she had wanted to find and hopefully experience herself.

Robin knew she wanted to live away from the group, so she found herself housing in Ahmedabad. She knew she wanted to learn about family health care, and so she found herself a doctor and a clinic in which to study. She wanted to understand more about meditation and the inner spirit, so she found a self-proclaimed swami. She was able to compare his verbal interest in spirituality with the quiet, humble, strong faith of her friend, Dr. Joshi. I felt proud of her. She had learned how to meet her personal needs, while at the same time feeling at home in India.

It had been hard to watch Penny. It had taken her a while to decide on a topic and to find a way to explore it. She would stay a couple of nights at the battered women's shelter and interview people there. Then she would come back, have a cigarette, listen to a tape, and lie out in the sun. She needed to balance her probings into intense feelings at the shelter with the relaxed freedom that she had as a visiting American college student. This was the first time she had written a paper based on more than just a collection of facts. She did have lots of data, but there was much more: there was her involvement in what she saw. She had experienced an array of puzzling feelings and was faced

with the question of how one writes both about the subject
and the subject's effect upon the writer.

All of these students—even Al, who had failed to find
his holy man—were doing their best to understand who
they were and what that meant for their relationship to
their world at home and the larger global society. Each was
working on a particular curiosity he or she had and experimenting with ways of exploring it. They were measuring
their ability to communicate effectively, dealing with
whatever response they got, and analyzing the answers
they came up with.

The potential of transcending one's cultural limitations lies in exactly this tangle of new impressions, past
assumptions, and future possibilities; it grows from this
confusion out of which meaning is made.[6] In this traffic of
explanations of human experience one may be able to find
a vehicle which helps illuminate how the world works and
what one's place in it is. In the end, immersion in its myriad
parts may help one grasp the sense of life's whole.

4

HOMESTAYS

After almost three months of living in Gujarat, we packed up our bags and headed for our two-week homestays. In the fall semester we went to Jodhpur, in the state of Rajasthan, northwest of Gujarat. In the spring we traveled southeast to Pune, in the state of Maharashtra. In both cases the students stayed separately, in homes of well-off families.

Each time we moved we became more understanding and appreciative of the place we had left, even if the change was a relief. This time was no exception. When we moved away from rural Sadra, from the simple living of the Gujarat Vidyapith, we were able to see the benefits of being so involved in life in the poor rural communities. Now as we encountered modern, wealthy Indian families, we carried with us a new group of stereotypes and expectations. At the same time we could look back, make comparisons, and continue to deepen our understanding of Indian life and our relation to it.

There was a feeling of great relief as the train left the Ahmedabad station. We were out of the restrictive environment of the Gujarat Vidyapith, traveling to luxurious homes with hot water, dining rooms complete with tables and chairs, beer, meat, cars, televisions. We had opportunities to explore the outlying areas, go on an overnight camel safari, visit the impressive Ajanta and Ellora Caves, and party at one family's second home in the mountains. That was the fun part. And the fact that it was fun was a source of an underlying uneasiness. The spring-semester students had just come from the worst riots yet in Ahmedabad. Twelve thousand people were in refugee camps, all transportation into the city had been shut down, and houses near the Vidyapith had been burned and looted. When we arrived in Pune, it was as though we had gone to a different country. The people around us had no idea what it had been like. The contrast was disturbing.

The families we stayed with had more similarities with our own at home. There were riding lessons, computer programming classes, golf games, refrigerators, televisions, furniture, Western dress. All of these caused the students to think carefully about Westernization and modernization; they reflected on the distinction between these people's lives and their own.

One of the first issues that the students ran into had to do with servants. Every family had a bevy of them: a night watchman, cook, driver, *dhobi* (laundry person), and perhaps someone to watch the children. The students felt particularly ambivalent about this arrangement. Our values of social equality, which had at least been mouthed at the Vidyapith, were challenged here, where servant and master roles were clear and set. Tania told us of one experience she had during dinner at her homestay. The salt shaker was on Tania's left, the youngest daughter was on her right. Tania was amazed when the daughter ordered the servant to fetch the salt when Tania could have easily passed it to her.

Geoff also had a run-in on the issue of servants. He started getting friendly with the driver in his family; he would say "thank you," smile, and carry his own luggage from the car. The sixteen-year-old son cautioned him not to be too friendly or the servant would soon think he was equal to his employers and consequently become difficult to manage. Robin also had struck up a mutual friendship with the servant woman in her house; she, too, was told to restrain herself, that servants must remember their place. Cindy commented on the way the boys in her family treated the servants, yelling at them, demanding they immediately drop their work and do the boys' bidding.

In discussing this later, we talked about what the servants do and how we handle that work in the United States. We drive our own cars; we usually cook our own dinners and clean our own homes, though some families do have domestic help; and many families have washers, driers, dishwashers, food processors, and vacuum cleaners. We come from a technological society that employs machines instead of people. We are able to avoid the stickiness of the employer-employee relationship, at least within our homes. Cindy went on to say that we, too, are dealing with questions raised by a mechanized workforce that leaves many people unemployed. In a country like India, with its large population, people need employment. We discussed the importance of being careful not to take on a self-righteous tone since our society is dealing with similar issues but in different forms.

The self-righteous tone was a form of judgment. We had just spent eleven weeks living with tribal people, villagers, and poor urban dwellers, and now we were confronted with the contrasting wealth of upper-class Indians. In some ways the students were even more critical of these families than of the poor. They expected and assumed them to be more like their own families, to hold similar values. The self-righteous tone came from a lack of understanding about the original forces that caused the caste/servant/master relationship and about the contemporary forces that maintain it. We enjoyed all the amenities available to us and felt uncomfortable with them at the same time. We had just come from a much simpler existence and felt as if we had landed in Rockefeller-like lifestyles, when really these homes were not so different from our own in America.

In Jodhpur Tania stayed with a royal family. They had been Maharajas up until 1947 when they were removed from power. In Pune, Geoff stayed with a family that owned much of the real estate in the city and ran the weekly newspaper as well. Although these people's lifestyles were not so different from those of the middle class in the United States, they were extremely well-off by Indian standards.

Another adjustment was to the difference in clothing. We had just recently come from an institution that required us to wear handspun, handwoven clothing; most Gandhians wore Indian styles—*kurta* (tunic) and *pajamas* (loose trousers, not nightclothes) for men; *salwar kameeze* (dress over drawstring pants) or saris for women. By the time we arrived at our homestays, most of our clothing had, shall we say, a well-used look. We had been washing our own clothes by hand and one could tell, by the slightly grey color, that we hadn't used Tide. We arrived looking rather dingy and wrinkled. Our hosts, on the other hand, were wearing the latest in Western styles. The young women wore tight-fitting Levis, heels, and T-shirts; the young men wore peg pants and denim jackets. Hairstyles were Westernized as well. All of the women in the countryside and many in Ahmedabad had long hair, a symbol of feminine beauty. In Pune, many young women wore their hair short. They were a shock to us and we were a shock to them. We were all terribly underdressed. Our host families, not fully aware of our former conditions, couldn't understand why Americans, who could afford to come all the way to India, would dress this way.

Each side looked at the other and saw some part of their own culture reflected back. We had come to study Gandhi; the students had been interested in traditional dance and music, folk songs, and crafts. The Indians we met here wanted to hear the latest Prince tape and played

Stevie Wonder, Michael Jackson, and Cindy Lauper at their parties. In some ways, we were bumping into one another's stereotypes once again. We both had preconceptions of what the other would look and be like, and we each felt trapped by the other's stereotypes.

In the course of the homestay, Daniel had to shift his image of Indian women. He had his first extended period of contact with Indian women in Jodhpur. During his time in Sadra and Ahmedabad and while preparing his ISP, he had mostly spent time with men. Now he was staying with a Sikh family that included a mother and a beautiful daughter, who struck him as the quintessential lovely Indian woman. She was soft-spoken, intelligent, articulate, tall, slender. She had long black hair and wore beautiful saris. Daniel developed a crush on her. She fit all his stereotypes.

One day, however, they were sitting at the dining room table, and she began to ask what kind of food he ate at home. She then went on to recount her husband's trip to Singapore, where he had gone to the wonderful, beautiful McDonald's restaurant and had enjoyed it immensely. Daniel's image of the quintessential Indian woman—with discriminating taste—fell apart as she went on to ask him if he had ever been to a McDonald's and expressed her fervent hope to do so sometime.

The students had come looking for traditional India and had found it in the villages of Sadra and Saurashtra, but here they were surprised to find a preponderance of Western influence. There was, however, an interesting distinction between Jodhpur and Pune. In Jodhpur the families were wealthy and they had modern conveniences, such as televisions, cars, perhaps a VCR, but they were more traditional and more aligned with Indian values and customs than the wealthy families in Pune, who were closer to Bombay and more influenced by Western culture. Penny experienced this combination of modern and traditional India at an anniversary party in Jodhpur:

The scene at the Palace unearthed memories I was sure I had permanently buried in my subconscious years ago. This was not only a déjà vu in setting or ambience; it triggered feelings so intense that for several hours I really felt as though I were reliving a painful part of my childhood.

Yes, how could I have forgotten! The stares I would receive when I would arrive. The dreaded "once-overs." I remember how self-conscious I was about my appearance. The boys were always grouped together at one side of the room and us girls stuck together at the other end. Though no one dared dance, the D.J. was there, hired for the whole evening. I always wondered what he thought about working for these parties where no one dared dance. Rather than making the room look more lively, the strobe lights only made it look bigger and more barren, especially with all the guests squished into the four corners of the room.

I was attending a party with educated, wealthy, well-traveled adults. All of the women who attended this lavish affair were my age or older, all married, and most of them mothers. Why were they sitting by themselves in one corner of the room? Why weren't they mingling with their husbands and their husbands' friends?

They were all trying so hard to be Western in terms of their manners and dress, but they couldn't do it. They got as far as emulating a seventh grader's bar mitzvah held in suburban New York. I started to feel guilty if I was talking too much with one man. I feared that his wife would be glaring at me and making accusations about me to her other female friends at the other side of the room. How could I forget the dirty looks I would get from that boy's "steady girl" if I was seen talking with him? It was seventh grade all over again.

I felt as though I was invited to this shindig to be the "icebreaker." No one else would go out on the dance floor—"Get the Americans to get the party rolling!" I'm no icebreaker at home, what makes them think that I will be one here? Though all present were full-fledged adults, they still had a hard time interacting with the opposite sex. It was Boy meets Girl all over again.

I understood this shyness when we were visiting villages, but I was astonished to find this in educated couples. It dawned on me that although the people I've met in Jodhpur all had the luxuries associated with the West, in terms of their apprehension in dealing with those of the opposite sex, they were as "traditional" as the villagers. I wrongly assumed that once you acquire many of the habits of the West, your attitudes will be sure to follow the same pattern. Though at the time I was disgusted with their "childish behavior," I realize now that this was because I was seeing their behavior in terms of my own past experiences. Upon reflection, I now think it was a refreshing sight to see that many of the educated and wealthy people are still able to adapt their newfound wealth into their old customs. Though it was seventh grade for me, it was 1984 for them and that is something I must not forget.

Susan also made discoveries about the nature of male-female relationships, particularly in marriages. From the start of the program she had questioned the apparent lack of freedom inherent in arranged marriages. In Sadra she had stayed with a family with three daughters and had been particularly sensitive to the youngest daughter's feeling of entrapment in both her father's and her future husband's homes. Susan's homestay in Jodhpur was in a large, joint family with thirty members, and she had an opportunity to explore the institution of marriage in some detail. She wrote:

> The institution of marriage has seemed a rather vague concept to me in the past several years, vague in the sense that a marriage in modern-day America hardly seems practiced and rarely seems to work out. In American society today, where the individual's rights and

freedoms are constantly being exercised and vigorously upheld, the institution of marriage has been forced to adapt and change. The results in America have been staggering, with 50 percent of marriages ending in divorce and the family structure severely weakened. In India, however, the individual is the one who's constantly changing and adapting and as a result, the institution of marriage and the family unit have never been stronger. I've gained insight and perspective on this during my two-week family homestay in Jodhpur.

My family was wealthy yet very traditional, and immediately upon meeting them my sympathy went out to the three women in the family. The plight of the Indian housewife has always made me uneasy and this was no exception. It never seemed fair, especially that first evening, that I should sit and eat with the men, with the women scurrying around serving us, always ready with that next chapati. And at first, I just couldn't overlook the injustices I saw. Why should the men sit on the couches and the women on the floor? Why should the men eat first and the women only after everyone had finished? Why should women be subservient and have to jump to their husbands' commands?

Afternoons I usually spent with the three women in their bedrooms. Away from their husbands and father-in-law they would let their hair down and talk, or rather let their saris down off their heads. (When in the presence of their fathers-in-law and in some cases husbands, women must cover their heads with their saris.)

"Walk slowly, speak softly, speak quietly," they'd say. "That is what a good Indian lady is like." "But why? Why should you have to speak slowly?" I'd ask. "We don't have to think about it anymore. We've been doing it since we were little." It didn't make sense to me and they couldn't explain it to me, but I've realized that that's an integral part of the answer. They couldn't answer my continuous "whys?" because "why" was something they never asked themselves. The attitude you bring to any task is the key to your satisfaction with it. I've realized this more and more recently. These Indian women have known, since their childhood, that they would speak slowly, walk slowly, and marry a man their father would pick for them and cover their heads in front of their fathers-in-law. And so to them, it's not upsetting and a hardship to be a traditional housewife, but rather a part of their life that they've accepted willingly and anticipated anxiously. What's more, in many cases, wives wouldn't care to change their set-up, even if they could.

We were driving along in the ambassador car (Indian model), three men in the front seat, three women in the back seat. "What's the difference between Indian life and American life?" Ravidra asked me. "Well, first of all, we'd never sit this way in a car with all the women in the back and all the men in the front. We'd all feel weird sitting like this." Everyone laughed. In the midst of our laughter, though, he stopped the car and moved into the back seat next to his wife and sent Abba into the front seat next to her husband. The men seemed quite happy with the new set-up, yet the women seemed a little uncomfortable.

From that day on, I started to see the marriage around me as much less of an instance of exploitation and much more of a prescribed give-and-take between husband and wife that made both parties extremely happy and which formed an incredibly solid family structure. I started to envy their set-up rather than be shocked by it. I realized that all the freedoms I enjoy also bring with them tons of responsibilities and tensions which form a different type of bondage in themselves.

I gained more respect for motherhood later that afternoon. As we sat chatting I was working determinedly on finishing my work journal and the women were knitting. I haven't knitted in maybe ten years, probably because I have spent most of those years poring over books and computers and preparing for exams and projects. And today what do I have? Yes, a lot of knowledge, but only with headaches and tension along the way. And today what do these women have? Sweaters and scarves that are a real product of creative energies.

I have no conclusions to draw from these experiences, except that there is another "practical" way to live and, now that I've seen it working, I think that achieving a synthesis of the good aspects of Indian and American culture is the greatest challenge that I will face in the near future.

Susan had entered Gochenour and Janeway's seventh stage, "Derive a self-sustaining and meaningful relationship within the host culture."[1]

David Hoopes speaks about this frame of mind on the intercultural learning continuum:

Selective adoption of new attitudes and behaviors can now occur as the individual consciously or unconsciously responds to characteristics encountered in the other culture which are felt to be useful or desirable to emulate. This may take the form of adjustment or adaptation with the practical aim of enabling the person to function more effectively in the other culture. It may also be that the individual finds aspects of the other cultural pattern simply more comfortable or satisfying in personal terms.[2]

The challenge that Susan articulated was exactly the task confronting everyone at this time. By the end of the homestay there were a mere five days left of the program. We headed for Delhi, where the students did last-minute shopping and sightseeing and where we conducted an evaluation of the program and each student's participation.

5

EVALUATION

We were at the end of the program. We started out in the village of Sadra, traveled even farther afield into the tribal area, lived in Ahmedabad for four weeks, had our own adventures around Gujarat, and brought the semester to a close with families who represented the beginning of our reentry into Western society. The students were not altogether happy about leaving the villages far behind and journeying back towards the United States. There was an undercurrent of anxiety as they contemplated returning to the pressures of living in modern America. Penny wrote this piece about our luxury bus ride from the homestays to our final destination in New Delhi:

> (DELHI: 130 KM) The terrain is the same. The flat farmland stretches on endlessly in front of me while the aroma emanating from the mustard seed plants attacks my senses from the open window behind me. The people still look the same—their once colorful lungi pants, turbans, skirts and saris are now soiled from the long day's work in the fields. The innumerable tea shacks scattered along the "highway" are filled with patrons squatting, in what appears to me a very painful position, as they sip their afternoon cha. Though I can't see, smell, or hear anything different, the feeling is unlike anything I've experienced before. I'm only going to New Delhi but I feel as though I'm

going home. Why do I want to hijack this Jaipur-New Delhi
express bus and turn back, back to the "real" India—the
India where there are no businessmen chattering in
English in the seats across the aisle; the India where Levis
on women is an exception, not the norm; the India where
all those simple, hardworking, yet incredibly hospitable
people live?

(DELHI: 90 KM) I'm scared. I will see opulence, elegance,
expensive cars and five-star restaurants. How will I deal
with that? I've been removed from the luxuries in life for
so long that now I'm worried I've forgotten how to act. I
suddenly feel all those anxieties I had in America resurfacing. I thought I had grown out of those anxieties about
my appearance and how I carried myself. I thought I was
no longer preoccupied with how others saw me. I thought
when I went through security at Kennedy Airport three
months ago that the x-ray machine zapped those feelings
out of me for good.

I suddenly feel fat. My hair needs a trim. I can't believe I've
been wearing these same ratty clothes for days on end.
Oh, how I wish I were back in some village in Gujarat,
whose name I can't pronounce correctly, sitting on one of
those oversize wood and canvas cots with a dozen or
more Indians, communicating only through song, dance
and laughter. Words, English words, have no formidable
place in that India.

(DELHI: 40 KM) Billboards are now advertising products
I would see along the road in the U.S. I see speed limit
signs—now that's a first! The reststop reminds me of the
Vince Lombardi Reststop on the New Jersey Turnpike.
There's a manicured lawn with picnic tables and swings;
the bathrooms have an attendant; and they serve
omelettes, pizza and milk shakes along with the vege-
table samosas and *papad*. Is this India?

This journey to India has taken me from one extreme to
another, and now back again. But maybe I don't want to
go back again. I do want to go home, but I don't want to
forget this other extreme. One day I was in New York and

the next I was in a remote village in the state of Gujarat. We didn't stop in New Delhi or Bombay—we were thrust right into the heart of India. But since then, we've been slowly heading towards bigger cities. Now I'm on my way to New Delhi, one of the biggest cities in India, and all I can think of is how I want to be back in that remote village. As this bus reaches the outskirts of the city, I can feel my heart pounding with anticipation and dread. If I can't go back to the villages right now, please don't let me forget them in the future. I always heard that before one dies, their entire life passes before their eyes. Though I'm certainly not dying, all of my experiences thus far seem to be resurfacing. I want to lock them in my memory and throw away the key. But they encompass too much to keep them all for myself. They must be shared with others.

Part of Penny's feeling was a fear of reentering the competitive, complex New York society from which she had come. Another large part was her awareness, as she contrasted the rural settings with the sprawling New Delhi metropolis, that those villages had something very special to offer her: hospitality, an enjoyment of human community, making music together, a basic acceptance of her despite her "ratty clothes and untrimmed hair." Finally, there was her fear of forgetting, of sinking back into the circumstances, roles, and mindsets from which she had come—a fear of losing all that she had gained—in the overwhelming hubbub of life in New York City. Penny needed reinforcement and support to be able to reenter and reintegrate.

Of course, the students were also looking forward to their return. There was much discussion about favorite foods and friends and about their families. They were eager to catch up on the latest movies, records, and political events. They wondered how they had changed, how they would feel, how people would see them, what had really happened for them on this trip. It was hard to predict from New Delhi; they would only really know when they were once again back in the milieu from which they had come. And, no doubt, the fabric of their lives at home had changed as well. Friends might have moved on and might be more emotionally distant. Perhaps the students would need to find new friends with whom to share some of their new interests and perceptions.

During our last five days in Delhi, we met in the mornings to evaluate the program as a whole. We examined what the students found to be most difficult and least valuable, as well as what was most worthwhile and enlightening. Sadra, which had seemed boring at the time, had become the anchor point for the trip. It was home in India. When Susan, Cindy, and Geoff returned to Gujarat during their independent travels, Sadra was where they visited. The relationships the group had made there were strong, partially because they were our first. Sadra was the arena in which we first tested our own assumptions, stereotypes, and romanticized images. The people of Sadra became real to us before others on the trip; we had the most constant, day-to-day interaction with them as well.

The most difficult part of the semester was the time spent in Ahmedabad, during the Life and Culture Seminar. The students' evaluations heavily stressed the need for more student participation in planning, more freedom to move around on their own, and more time to get involved in the community, which had yielded so much rich information outside of the classroom. As Daniel wrote:

> I have gained a greater understanding of India's politics, economics, religion and social customs by being with and talking to those people whose lives are the products of all these forces. The Life and Culture Seminar was most useful when it allowed for this informal dialogue between Indians and Americans, in other words, when it got us out of the Vidyapith campus and into the real world of Gujarat.

Other students felt this as well and, in retrospect,

appreciated the exposure to the wide variety of people they had encountered. Angela wrote:

> The greatest thing I learned is that India is a real country—I've seen it, so it's no longer fantasy. The differences in lifestyle that I had heard about are here, though they often look different than I thought they would because I see their place in the whole way of life. Having seen India from village to city, by living with people of all different backgrounds, I have a concept of India as a whole. It's hard to believe Delhi and Saurashtra are in the same country, but the realization that they are is an important one. Or that an arranged marriage may be great, a satisfying way of arranging your life; that khadi employs three million people; that tea sellers are sometimes the holiest people, not *sannyasis*. There's just too much to put down, but I feel like I've gotten some feel for India as a land and culture and people.

The importance of having seen these parts of India only came fully into focus upon our contact with other Westerners who were tourists in Rajasthan and New Delhi. Cindy wrote in her evaluation:

> The best part of the Life and Culture Seminar was the exposure to the "real" India we received, that is, the 75 percent of India which is rural and agriculturally based. I appreciate this more and more as I see the alternative way of seeing India—staying in tourist hotels with Western comforts or seeing the sights, e.g., Jaisalmer, Agra, etc., and missing out on the small villages, and family life of the country.

During the evaluation of the Life and Culture Seminar, students also expressed the importance of developing a deeper understanding of different modes of learning. Angela wrote insightfully:

> There are two levels of learning involved in the Life and Culture Seminar—or rather, one of learning and one of

understanding. The one level of learning includes things possible to learn in America—things that are factual, descriptive, deductive. In the second level, you may not be able to express more, but you have seen what could be described and it is real for you. In both areas this trip to India has increased my knowledge enormously. The second aspect is the one I value more; I think one of the only ways I have been able to express this is through my poetry. But I have been getting a feeling for the rhythms of life, for the land—India is an amazingly beautiful country. There is something special in the quality of the light, in the people and why they live like they do, what they like and why.... It's vague to try to say that, but it's hard to say more than that India has become a real land and culture to me, one I love and respect. My time in India has been fun, often difficult, challenging, uncomfortable, yes, but I have kept being willing to try new ways of doing things or thinking of things. Those encounters have been exciting. I may not adopt all—or any—of the methods and thoughts when I return to America (though I probably will!), but the comparison of the cultures, the fact of having tried a different way of living and thinking will always be with me.

Daniel also spoke about the learning process and the significance of seeing India in a different light, from a less analytical and more impressionistic perspective:

I attribute my increased sensitivity of cultural surroundings to something I call aesthetic sense; the ability to look at events as if they were paintings or plays, regarding beauty, ugliness, form and pattern rather than quantifiable data. I cannot say how this aesthetic sense developed; all I can remember is a sudden feeling of being surrounded environmentally by richness and tradition, whereas before this crucial point, I could not grasp the holistic differences between East and West.

It is this kind of insight, this visceral comprehension and absorption of another culture that makes cross-cultural learning so important. We can only learn a limited amount about India through books, films, and other media. Only by meeting a new culture or country with all your senses alert can it become real, tangible, palpable—something that can burrow into and become an integral part of us.

It is not enough, however, to just go. As Robert Hanvey says:

> It is not easy to attain cross-cultural awareness or understanding of the kind that pushes you into the head of a person from an utterly different culture. Contact alone will not do it. There must be a readiness to respect and accept, and a capacity to participate. The participant must be reinforced by rewards that matter to the participant. And the participation must be sustained over long periods of time. Finally, one may assume that some plasticity in the individual, the ability to learn and change, is crucial.[1]

It was just this kind of multidimensional aspect of the program that made it so difficult to evaluate academically. As Elizabeth Warner says:

> Traditional ways of assessing cognitive knowledge (e.g., quizzes, examinations, papers, formal presentations) are not adequate for evaluating an individual learner's total experiential growth. We need techniques for assessing personal growth and maturity that address themselves in an integrated manner to the thoughts, feelings, and actions of the learner.[2]

We needed to find some way that would assess the experiential aspects of the learning. For instance, the language course consisted of more than learning Gujarati; the challenge was to learn how to communicate the best one could, using spoken language as well as nonverbal cues. The course stressed the need to be willing to extend oneself and to listen carefully so as not to jump to conclusions too quickly about what was being said or conveyed.

The Methods and Techniques in Field Study course, though the class with the least number of credits and fewest number of formal lectures, was the one activity that the students were always involved in. As Penny said, "I feel the real course began right when we got off the plane. We were, in fact, on one big 'drop-off,' dealing with strangers, finding out the unknown, and making mistakes." This course developed the ability to recognize one's own culturally colored biases as well as building skills in cross-cultural research and observation. Angela remarked on her final evaluation:

> Inevitably, by living in a culture you are doing field study—the difference is how conscious you are of the information you get, its implications and relation to other information. I realized how much you can learn by observing carefully—not only actions but emotions, not only listening but catching inflections and how people interact. If you combine this with deduction and analysis you can build up points of reference by which you can then interpret other observations.

The Life and Culture Seminar obviously involved much more than lectures and papers; it encompassed the trips to the tribal areas, Anand University, and Saurashtra, not to mention the homestays. During those experiences the students had a number of different kinds of assignments designed to help them articulate the learning that took place. They developed questionnaires and interviewed people. They wrote critical incident papers that described a particular event and what it taught them. They did role plays, wrote stream-of-consciousness papers, and discussed what they were learning. All these forms of expression contributed to their awareness of what they had learned and helped them articulate what they were seeing. The assignments also stimulated their thinking about their own lives.

And finally, the Independent Study Project was more than the final paper or product. It was an in-depth experience, involving much risk taking, coordinating, communicating, and synthesizing. They had kept work journals on the development of their projects since the beginning of the semester, tracking their initial ideas and continuing to record their thoughts, reactions, and insights as they went along. They also had a project advisor to help them in thinking through plans. These tools were useful in the final, most difficult task of assigning grades.

The students had a choice of getting grades or pass/fail marks. Either one was accompanied by a short paragraph written by me about the student's performance in each course. We were all confronted with the question of how one assesses the learning that has taken place, how one gives a "C" to someone who has been through so much. I felt that if grades and a short paragraph were all one had to show for an intense three and one-half months of twenty-four-hour attendance, then those grades had to give credit for experience itself. Although I was ultimately responsible for the final decisions on grades, I asked students to grade themselves before we met for private conferences.

One student decided that she didn't want grades but preferred the pass/fail marks instead. She felt that experience could not be judged. She had come to India to involve herself in a totally different society and she was learning night and day. That kind of learning, she said, should not be minimized or simplified by the final summation of a grade. She had come from an Ivy League university and had been purposefully experimenting with directing her own learning rather than just going along with the assignments for academia's sake.

As the week progressed and the other students were writing their evaluations and assessing their work, she started to rethink her position. By the end, she changed her mind. She reasoned that universities don't take pass/fail marks as seriously as they do traditional grades. The learning that gets assessed on a pass/fail basis is devalued. She realized that she felt strongly about what she had learned, about the way of life that was not planned to the last detail, that was more spontaneous and responsive. She felt it to be highly relevant not only to her life but to American society at large. She wanted to give recognition and credit to the experience and wanted her university to do the same, and so she chose to work with their symbols and requested grades.

What about students who did not have such clear insights, who had had a harder time? Should these differences be graded hierarchically? This came up in Al's case. He had gone to the tribal area equipped with names of contacts and some money. He journeyed farther away than anyone, both literally and figuratively. He, however, did not accomplish his task, nor did he change his focus while there in a way that would have educationally made the most of a difficult situation. He came back and wrote a paper based on library research and an interview. He learned about the Dang people but not by interacting with them. What grade should he get? "A" for effort? "C" for writing an inadequate paper? Or "B" for actually going so far, attempting, and in the end realizing that he had been a victim of his own expectations? The question was really this: What did he think he had learned? How could that be measured? Should that be measured?[3]

The period of evaluation was not finished until we brought out and reviewed the students' first comments on why they had wanted to come to India. Each student read his or hers aloud and then followed up with remarks about specific experiences and what they meant. I was surprised to find that, in some ways, this was a bit anticlimactic. The reports on the ISPs in Ahmedabad had been a time when students shared what they had learned, both outwardly and inwardly. There had also been numerous informal discussions, both as a group and in twos and threes, where the students reflected back over the program, its pros and cons, what they had gained, how they had changed, what returning to the States would be like or traveling on in India as a few planned to do. The last three weeks of the program had given them sufficient opportunity to reflect upon the semester.

Their hopes and fears had been spoken to in one way or another. They had all gotten more or less sick, they had been stared at, been bored, felt isolated, felt stereotyped, and been worried about the stability of relationships with friends back home. They had had moments of feeling overwhelmed with India's problems: the poverty, the riots, the overpopulation. And they had experienced the materialization of their fears and it hadn't been the end of the world.

Many had fulfilled their goals in coming; others had revised them after getting a more realistic picture of what was possible in the Indian environment. A few students had hoped that they would return with a clearer sense of their roles in the world. Robin and Tania came away very clear about their future career goals. Robin decided to go into health-care planning. Tania saw a long career ahead in the field of land reform and social justice. Susan and Angela, who had already chosen their directions, now had more material to work with—Angela had felt a sense of history in the Saurashtra villages that she hadn't found in Europe. Susan experienced a whole new mode of living, one that was more responsive to the moment. She would be traveling for another six months before returning to her high-powered computer job and Ivy League college. Daniel, though not clear on his career plans, felt that he had finished one era in his life: "I look back now at this as the closing chapter in one episode of my life and also the beginning of the next one."

Daniel and Margaret had both wanted to meet "holy people" and to experience some of the essence of Eastern philosophy and religion. Both went through the walls of their romanticized images and came out the other side with a finer sense of discrimination and a deeper appreciation for the wisdom and wonder embodied in people who did not necessarily consider themselves to be spiritual.

Penny had expressed a hope that she would find a way of being in India that would transcend the label of "American." She and others wanted the cultural barriers to melt. They wanted to find the similarities that transcend cultures, as though afraid of the differences that are used to separate cultures. By the end, they were much more familiar, though not necessarily more comfortable, with differences between themselves and their Indian counterparts. They also became more aware of the differences among Indians themselves.

As the program closed, the students could truly appreciate the depth and breadth of learning they had undertaken. They learned about themselves and their own negotiable and nonnegotiable values. Most importantly, however, they began to grasp the meaning of synthesis, the synthesis of individual needs and social responsibility, of objective and subjective modes of research, of traditional and modern ways to live. They no longer looked for exclusive conclusions but rather sought explanations that embraced the often contradictory realities that India holds within herself.

6

IMPLICATIONS

Discoveries

What are the implications of this college semester abroad program in India? What did we learn? What is transferable to other cross-cultural endeavors? What is the significance of the students' experiences and their reflections?

What I found to be most significant was participating in the students' work of untangling the web of confusing signals, outside demands, and personal interests which beset them. I watched them as they reached down into themselves to find an identity with which they could be comfortable and at home. They needed to learn how to care for themselves so that, after a period of renewal, they could once again go out and encounter difference and cope with the unknown. I accompanied them in their effort at deeper self-definition.

From the very first day all of them had been open and had spoken of wanting to learn, to better understand social conditions, and to find a way to play a part. They agreed to be learners, to admit they didn't know all the answers, to accept being wrong on occasion, to appear incomplete, ridiculous, and ignorant. This willingness to ground their pride, self-worth, and self-substantiation on the precept of growth and change allowed for movement. It helped them communicate better, listen carefully, and express themselves more accurately. It made them receptive to transformation from one point of view to another, from one level of understanding to another.

The following is a list of skills or qualities that I believe facilitate cross-cultural learning and adaptation. They are derived from my own experience and from observing as the students experimented and explored ways to meet this new world and maintain some sense of integrity at the same time:

1. Ability to live with ambiguity.

2. Maintenance of an inner control even when unable to control external circumstances.

3. Resourcefulness and creativity—the ability to be flexible, to take advantage of the unexpected. Cindy comments, "I found that my personal excursions into the culture gave me more insight into the Indian way of life. Many of the field trips were enjoyable, not because of the program but because of the incidents that were not programmed."

4. Detachment from a particular form, approach, or perspective without losing track of one's objective (but even being willing to question that). Margaret's experience was a good example. At one point she thought that her ISP would take a particular form but then had to totally revamp it while keeping her original intention in mind.

5. Ability to feel confident and capable without the benefit of outside props or people.

6. Sense of humor and willingness to play—a very important coping method.

7. Willingness to be vulnerable, to appear ridiculous in the eyes of others. "Above all, hang on to your sense of humor, don't take yourself too seriously, don't be embarrassed by anything they're not embarrassed about (i.e., shitting in a field with half a village for an audience)."

8. Adaptability to cultural ways, ability to learn languages—both verbal and nonverbal, and the ability to consciously choose when to adopt one cultural way over another.

9. Ability to accept one's own "negative" feelings, such as anger, frustration, irritation, disappointment, defeat, and to see them as flags, signposts, indicators of an opportunity to learn about cultural differences.

10. Ability to suspend judgment during a difficulty long enough to begin asking questions. The ability to not take things too personally.

11. Ability to question one's own values when they are challenged and yet not to let them go if, in the balance, they still remain right for oneself.

12. Ability to express oneself in some mode, to have some way to communicate one's impressions and to share joy cross-culturally by singing, playing music, writing poetry, or juggling.

13. Genuine love for human beings, the ability to see the light in all (including oneself). The willingness to accept people even if their behavior causes problems.

14. Curiosity, honoring the "quester within." Staying aware of and being in touch with that which motivates from deep inside, as it is the key to a richer understanding of both the new and the familiar cultures.

15. Love of adventure and challenge. Maintaining a healthy balance between growth and safety.

16. Impatience or intolerance for one's own lengthy periods of self-pity, self-doubt, and self-depreciation.

17. Perspective—a sense of the cycles of emotions, one's own patterns, the long-term and the short-term. The ability to detach from a situation, to step back and take ten deep breaths.

These skills are useful in most avenues of life but are particularly valuable in a cross-cultural setting. As the students' experiences testified, there is an inherent satisfaction in allowing these qualities to grow and flourish. As Abraham Maslow says:

> The achievement of self-actualization paradoxically makes more possible the transcendence of self, and of self-consciousness and of selfishness. It makes it easier for the person to merge himself as a part in a larger whole than himself.[1]

As the students followed the "impulses of their inner core,"[2] as they made decisions that promoted growth, they learned more and expanded outward. They were able to grasp the realities and understand the perspectives of others. For example, by spending day after day in the hut of her master puppet carver, Cindy's gut-level comprehension of and appreciation for the tensions and pleasures in his life increased. Her body, emotions, and mind now know that scene and because she was there to learn, because she went open and grateful for his time, the bond of mutual appreciation transformed her stay from a physically difficult, potentially alienating experience (because of a multitude of flies, cramped quarters, unsanitary food) into one of meaning and connection. She has been changed by that interaction. India's population of 750 million people is no longer just a statistic or a mass of people for Cindy but a multitude of individuals, one of whom is Govindji, the craftsman.

Susan found Sashi, the dancer, and his family; Robin connected with Dr. Joshi at the hospital; Eric befriended the Solomon family in the Jewish community; Ed learned from the Gandhian principal and his family; Margaret grew close to the women at the Jain ashram. Each student found some kind of meaningful, often loving relationship within the culture we had come to explore. Developing this kind of bond is often central to cross-cultural learning. The relationships did not always come easily, however. The stronger relations were those built on mutual give and take, the sharing of intense experiences. The more the students gave of themselves, the more they received and the deeper the connection.

The fact that the students found models for their own development in India, a different culture, automatically wove that country into the fabric of their lives. The students not only learned skills and broadened world-views, they also learned that all cultures offer some insight into what it means to be a human being.

Their more negative experiences contributed to further understanding human nature as well. All encounters with Indians were not rosy. All significant relationships were not easy. Our rather rigid guide on the trip to Anand taught the students a great deal though they may not have enjoyed every minute.

The country is now in their psyches, in their bodies, amoebas and all, not just because they traveled to another geographical space but because they went hungry with questions and devoured experiences to satisfy that hunger.

Throughout the semester a number of students had wanted to help more, to have an impact. They did, though not always in the way they anticipated. Eric's interest in the Jewish community caused them to become more con-

scious of themselves, helped them take a look at themselves from the outside. Penny and Susan's laughter brought
a welcome break to the Vidyapith students' routine lives in
Sadra. Tania's interest in organizing gave Kirtee (her project director) a chance to verbalize thoughts he had just
begun to formulate. Sometimes our willingness to learn is
more useful to a culture than our plans for helping. A Peace
Corps report makes this point:

> Filipinos with their incessant hospitality and curiosity,
> repeatedly made it plain that for them the main job of
> Peace Corps volunteers was to enjoy themselves and to
> enhance pleasure for those around them.... Nothing was
> more difficult for volunteers to understand or accept
> than that the Filipinos wanted them for pleasure in rela-
> tionships and not to achieve the tasks to which they had
> been assigned.[3]

The students were often literally helpful as well, but it
was their interest and willingness to ask questions and
listen to the answers (and in so doing, acknowledging
people's existence) that made the impact. Their willingness
to receive was a kind of gift that they gave. As Robert Kegan
says, "It is our recruitability, as much as our knowledge of
what to do once drawn, that makes us of value in our caring
for another's development."[4]

The implications of this for the students' understanding of international relations are interesting. These students grew up in the mid-sixties at the peak of U.S. power,
with the predominant idea that the United States was
number one in the world, with no needs, only surpluses.

For the students to travel to a seemingly "needy"
Third-World country and to discover that they (the students) have something to gain from that culture, opens
them to a potentially fundamental shift in their concept of
the nature of First- and Third-World relationships. India
may not have a computerized banking system, for example,

but it does have something to teach us. From *Habits of the Heart:*

> Perhaps life is not a race whose only goal is being fore-most. Perhaps the truth lies in what most of the world outside the modern West has always believed, namely that there are practices of life, good in themselves, that are inherently fulfilling.[5]

This is the lesson Susan learned in her homestay with the extended family in Jodhpur and what Daniel found on his pilgrimage. *Habits of the Heart* continues:

> We will need to remember our poverty. We have been called a people of plenty, and though our per capita GNP has been surpassed by several other nations, we are still enormously affluent. Yet the truth of our condition is our poverty. Our material belongings have not brought us happiness. Our military defenses will not avert nuclear destruction. It would be well for us to rejoin the human race, to accept our essential poverty as a gift and to share our material wealth with those in need.[6]

Our Effect on Those in the Host Society

What are the implications of this type of experience for the Indians? How are they affected by our process of growth and learning? Are we in danger of using other cultures, once again, for our own personal needs, this time taking personal growth and cross-cultural awareness instead of cotton and tea? Are we exploiters or imperialists unconscious of the consequences of our learning? Yes and no.

In Sadra the bulk of the village people, with whom we had little interaction, were aware of us but we were not aware of them. They were invisible to us as individuals, but we were present for them. They were transformed into objects by our cameras: we took photos of the "Indian woman bearing brass water vessel" or the "malnourished child playing in the dirt." Every semester the village people are exposed to groups of Americans who come to town. We buy clothes, baubles, candy, jewelry, sodas; take pictures; sometimes give money to children; sometimes stop for tea as guests of the doctor, novelist, grocer, and accountant. We seldom go to the homes of untouchables or unskilled laborers. The villagers encounter constant, but brief, exposure to the tourist side of the Americans. On the other hand, the families who meet the students on village visits get just as much chance to examine us, ask, look, and wonder, as we do with them. They have the opportunity to learn a little more about the world beyond their village by talking with us and looking at our things—by hosting us.

Some of the students felt that the continual arrival of a new group of American students every semester was hard on the Vidyapith students, particularly in the realm of male-female friendships, which were sometimes more important to the Indian student than to the American woman. The need to choose which society's standards to adopt was a challenge to the students, particularly on the sensitive subject of men and women. The American students were unmarried; they had relationships with the opposite sex in the United States. They had to decide whether they wanted to relate to the opposite sex in their American way or not, knowing that if they did, it would have a totally different meaning than in the United States. Susan questioned whether she should write to Jagdesh, a G.V. student, after she returned home. She worried that it might contribute to illusions he had of being able to start a restaurant with her in New York. She felt bad about having raised his expectations that would be let down once she had gone home. It is, once again, the question of "being themselves." Behavior that would have been perceived one way in the States would have been interpreted differently in India.[7]

Other Vidyapith students complained that American students would take pictures and promise to send copies to them but never follow through. This was true. They would find after three more months of experience that they had a multitude of pictures that needed copying and sending and become overwhelmed by the extent to which they had obligated themselves, forgetting or not wanting to think about how important it might be for the people back in India. On the other hand, sometimes the American students felt manipulated into picture taking. Indians couldn't understand that, relative to a student's budget, it costs a lot to get extra prints made. They felt a bit taken advantage of, especially by those who were not close friends.

The upshot was that one or the other of the parties felt used by the other. Some of the Indians wanted the status that they perceived came from having Americans in their homes. They wanted access to America, photos, sponsorship, names of universities, money, and things that they could not get themselves. Americans wanted experience with poverty, a folk culture, craft items, photographs of "strange" things to show to friends. We partook of people's hospitality; they partook of us. Sometimes our hosts wanted more time than we could spare. It was interesting that we did not get this feeling as frequently in poorer families as much as in upwardly mobile families who saw our visit as a potential steppingstone, and as a symbol of all that is desirable, such as wealth, technology, and status.[8]

The other area of student insensitivity came over the use of money. Most Indians with whom we were in contact had very little money. I felt particularly self-conscious when the students would freely spend the day's wages of a laborer on a package of peanuts or cheese and gobble it down without sharing it with all others around, without being conscious of the many watching eyes. It's not just

Westerners who do this; certainly wealthier Indians do so as well, but the students were not always aware that not everyone we were with could buy a soda or a rickshaw ride any time they wished. Sometimes this lack of awareness put our Indian friends in the uncomfortable position of having to shell out more than they could afford. In India people seldom split the bill. One person will often treat those around. American students were recipients of that generosity but, at the beginning, were much slower to see the appropriateness of reciprocating. They went on the assumption that everyone could buy his or her own.

The students were learning the culture and were picking up many cues to guide their behavior. But they were still operating under American financial assumptions, particularly as they were extremely advantageous for us. The dollar:rupee ratio was 1:12; one dollar equaled twelve rupees. Minimum wage for male laborers was ten rupees per day (eight rupees for women). In some cases it didn't make sense to restrain ourselves. When we were buying gifts for friends at home, for instance, we could spend freely; we were benefiting the Indian economy. But we put a wedge into our relationships with our less solvent Indian friends if we spent too liberally in their presence.

The students learned a lot about how to be in Indian culture and how to get along. That they connected well with people and could identify with them did not mean that they had completed the process of acculturation. They were there for only three and one-half months; they had a long way to go before being able to act with the "awareness of how another culture feels from the standpoint of the insider."[9]

Stereotyping

In his book, *Notes on India*, Robert Boehm talks about the exploitation of Indians by Western hippies who come to

India looking for a guru.[10] Margaret came close to this with her assumption that she could understand Jainism merely by taking on the outward forms of being a nun, like wearing a white sari and carrying a begging bowl. Her fantasies about "freaking out" her parents on return and telling her friends at home of her exotic adventures verged on the disrespect and simplification that Boehm was referring to. She escaped that, however, by persevering through the collapse of her fantasies and by approaching the nuns with a genuine interest in why they had chosen this life.

Certainly everyone had their stereotyped images of what India would be like—exotic India with elephants, camels, gypsies, snake charmers, tigers, swamis, maharajas, immortalized Gandhians, open markets, Hindi films, dancers, enlightened masters, coconuts, beaches, Himalayas, and the holy Ganges. All these are real and yet for the students they were symbols, representing mystery, ultimate wisdom, ultimate sensuality, ultimate poverty, life, death, love, hatred. India is full of paradoxes and contradictions; it represents all aspects of humanity. We don't have these same symbols in the States (though we do have Disneyland, New York, Silicon Valley, Las Vegas, and Hollywood—all of which some Indians see as symbols of qualities they find missing in their lives). The images surrounding these symbols often provided the initial magnetism that drew the students from their own culture to India.

The danger lay in mistaking our images for reality and refusing to allow the country to be more than our projections. I found it very important to break these images, see something new, see complexity instead of grasping for pat answers that made us feel safe. Each time a stereotype was cracked, another stereotype was less apt to take its place. We became familiar with the feel of frozen perceptions breaking up.

We dealt with stereotypes as a group by starting from where we were. Each time we encountered an exotic aspect of India, we would take it on—we went on that camel safari, we went to the beach, we met a maharaja. And each time we did that, we learned and went way beyond the motivating image. We learned about the working lives of camel drivers; we found a shipwrecking yard at the beach where we had imagined palm trees and white sand; the maharaja explained the changes in political structures since his father's time and described what that meant for him and his family. Exotic India became a jumping-off spot, not something to be denied but to be explored. In the exploring we moved through to a deeper understanding.

I say deeper, hoping the reader will know that there is always deeper to go. The students had been in India for one brief semester, and there was a slight danger in their thinking they understood it all now that they had spent some time there and had met a variety of Indians. Those that left knowing they were at a plateau of knowledge, knowing they had only begun to discover what they didn't know, were the ones who'd really grasped the complexity of the society. Of course we all made generalizations and we all learned more than we knew when we began. But to speak definitively of a country like India, which is such an assortment of cultures, is to have missed the point.

The students had accomplished some remarkable things during their time in India: 12,000 miles away from their homes, they had come to love and respect people of a different color, economic background, religious belief system, and family structure, and had come to know themselves better in the process. By being in India during Mrs. Gandhi's assassination and the riots in Ahmedabad, they understood better some of the reasons for separation, for conflict and war. They had come to see how fear can ignite fires and greed can explode bombs. They had learned from the Indians who became their friends and from the ones with whom they had had difficulties. The culture as a whole—the land, the geography, climate, animals, movement in the villages and cities—all were teachers.

These twelve students will not necessarily go out and save the world. But the experience that they had, of entering a different society and of discovering so much about themselves and about India, had its impact. All of their "ahas," insights, and perceptions are now part of them. They've begun to learn what contributes to better, clearer communication, and what interferes. They know a little bit more about the cultural lenses through which they peer. They know a little bit more about who they are individually, what they want, and what they have to give. They have an inkling that the world is full of cultures that not only have different languages and economic and political structures, but that feel and think differently. They have experienced a particular gestalt, a unique living mosaic that they will miss when they leave and which beckons to them to return.

APPENDIX 1

Life of an Academic Director

The students were not the only ones to go through culture shock. I, too, went through a series of stages and cycles within those stages. I came with my own expectations, images, stereotypes, hopes, assumptions, and values. My focus, though, was much more on the students' experience than it was on my own exploration of India.

My task was to integrate my goals with what was expected of me by the American institution, the Gujarat Vidyapith, and the students, all of whom had slightly different needs and expectations.

First of all, what did I want? I, perhaps unrealistically, wanted the students to break through crystallized patterns and then come out a little more integrated with themselves, and with a stretched consciousness about who else shares this planet. I wanted them to begin to understand their own culture and their own personalities as they made their way into Indian society. I wanted the students to connect with Indians. I wanted them to remember people whose opinions were important to them, people to whom they had entrusted their vulnerability. I wanted them to leave India with a multitude of memories, but without the ability to wrap the experience neatly in words, to know that there was something still indescribable and unavailable to the analytical mind, but lodged and present, now permanently a part of them. I hoped they would begin to feel comfortable with ambiguity, to not need answers, and to enjoy the questioning. I hoped they would feel homesick for India when they returned to the States. I wanted them to feel that something was missing when they got off the plane. I wanted them to find and nourish that spark in themselves that would push them and guide them in their explorations both in India and beyond.

The institution for which I worked had a broad expectation of the academic director as detailed in the job description:

> The academic director must be attuned to the educational philosophy and expectations of the School and possess both commitment to academic excellence and the personal qualities required by the program. Among the latter are cultural sensitivity and adaptability, infectious intellectual curiosity and enthusiasm for challenge; tact and diplomacy in working with host nationals, on the one hand, and American students, on the other; organizational ability; energy; and sense of humor.[1]

The school was particularly concerned with maintaining a "rigorous academic program" so that it would continue to be recognized by American universities and colleges. In addition, it was concerned with the students' reactions and relationship with the Gujarat Vidyapith since, in the recent past, students had had problems with Vidyapith rules and requirements. The school wanted to be sure that I would be able to be diplomatic, while protecting the students' interests. That particular task turned out to be one of the most challenging of all.

The Gujarat Vidyapith expected me to be a leader, a decision maker for the students, and it expected me to make the students cooperate and obey the rules and requirements. I was to make sure the students wore khadi while on campus, that they attended spinning and prayer on time, that they did not bring any meat or eggs on campus (as had happened previously). I was to know of their whereabouts at all times and was responsible for keeping them in line if they started acting in a manner inappropriate for the G.V. As for the students, they expressed their expectations of me in writing during orientation:

> Be a friend and advisor, take the initiative to criticize us if you feel we are acting incorrectly, but also let us make our own mistakes, understand that we will make mistakes, and be able to laugh at them with us.

> Be willing to allow us to study what we want within the context of the program, e.g., something besides Gandhian goals and philosophy; respect our efforts and problems, conclusions and opinions; allow us to think through problems for ourselves instead of presenting a solution; explain the rationale for work that might seem pointless if we can't see the end.

> Understand that this is the first time many of us have ventured out of the country and help us with our initial problems and tell us that "it's all right to feel that way" but that "we'll get over it"; understand that we may feel, at some point or another, that we must be alone to think about things and to put them in perspective; push us in the direction that we think we are interested in pursuing.

> Be involved with the group on both an even level and as a superior as the situation demands; provide information and a source of maturity at times when we need it to pull ourselves along.

The combination of these different expectations, the fact that I was also new to the job and new to the Gujarat Vidyapith made the first semester an experiment in "living creatively in the unknown" for me as well. As is true in all teaching, I was both a learner and a teacher. And, as is also the case in all teaching, the challenge was to act with right timing, to be sensitive to the various forces at hand, and to be able to make judgments about when to introduce certain subjects for discussion. It was also necessary to know when and how to raise questions, when to call students on culturally inappropriate action, and particularly how to work with the students in a way that would increase their understanding and awareness, enabling them to encounter any situation and be able to learn from it rather than being either defeated or lulled into inactivity by it.

As I've described, the students were not always happy. They were busy bumping into their own cultural limitations. The lack of freedom in the program; being stereotyped by Indians; feeling isolated in the group; worrying about their ISP project, the riots, the lack of word from friends at home; feeling frustrated by the difficulty of communicating; and being disappointed and angry with the Vidyapith for not being a model of Gandhian ways all contributed to their sense of discomfort. I continually needed to investigate the origin of the disgruntlement and to be clear, myself, on where responsibility lay.

Robert Kegan, once again, suggests that people are in a constant movement between being embedded in a psychological frame of reference that is either primarily inclusive (part of a group) or autonomous (independent of groups). When persons are moving from one stage to another they need that which they are leaving or rejecting to remain long enough to push against it. They need to become separate from where they have just come and then, eventually, to reintegrate in a way that has new meaning. My role was both as agent, to assist in leaving the home environment and in entering into India, and as helper, to make that an enriching experience.[2]

I also ended up in a role that embodied all the good aspects of community living along with the negative aspects of personal limitation. I could be useful as group coordinator, monitor of the group feeling, and also as facilitator for each student's sojourn into his/her own realm of exploration and expression.

During the first semester, when the students had become passive and eventually angry, my dilemma was figuring out whether I should try to relieve those feelings by changing something in the program or whether I should allow the students their feelings, listen, and accompany them in finding a way to make the best of it.

What needed changing was always debatable: students, program, or approach. Yet, as director of the program, I often felt their dissatisfaction was partially my responsibility because, in fact, there were aspects of the program that could be improved, and I recognized my own limitations.

I knew that entering a culture was a process, but I only knew it through my own experience. At the beginning of the first semester I found that I was elated with the students' absorption and involvement: "I find myself enjoying their wide-eyed openness to the water buffaloes, to the waving wheat and wandering pigs." Then as a few weeks went by, I found myself getting impatient with them. I wrote in my journal, "I expect insights and more 'ahas.' I dislike the superficial objectifying that goes on from all sides. But it's too early, I'm pushing the process. I'm impatient. They need a period of time not to analyze, but to just absorb."

When we moved into Ahmedabad and the students found the library and felt the excitement of being in the city, I was confused: "They said that in Sadra they felt dead, unstimulated, dull, cut off, numb, frustrated." I was disturbed that despite their village visits and contact with the Indian students, they only now felt they were in India. They were finally in a mode (academic) that included books and English speakers they could understand; therefore, they felt they had arrived. I was perplexed about why they seemed not to have been touched by seeing how the majority of people live in India. As it turned out later, they had been affected quite deeply.

As we entered into the academic portion of the program, the Life and Culture Seminar, I found myself in the tenuous position of not actually being in charge of the lectures and visits. I made requests for speakers in the areas in which the students were interested. The Vidyapith staff and I went over the categories we had chosen and discussed possible lecturers and sites to visit. The arranging, however, was out of my hands. I was, therefore, not always able to tell the students exactly what to expect. More often than not, plans went awry. A lecturer wouldn't show; or if he did, he might be quite dull. I was as frustrated as the students at some points about not having very much control over our program. This was due, in part, to the high turnover of American academic directors in the program and the likelihood that they would not know the language. The Vidyapith's solution to that instability was to control the schedule, allowing me room to comment but not always room to make changes.

I, too, had to learn how to cope creatively with a change in the schedule and not become too attached to a plan. I felt the pressure of the academic requirements on my shoulders, so I needed to be ready with makeshift lectures or seminars. I had to learn to remain relatively calm and yet firm with the Vidyapith and clear about our needs, while simultaneously explaining to the students that, because of planning, we couldn't just drop one thing and do something else; we had commitments to others.

Sometimes I wondered if the program would work more smoothly if there was not an academic director. I often felt like a go-between; the students might have learned about the society more directly by working with the Vidyapith staff themselves.

Another consequence of being a middle-person was that I felt particularly aware of and responsible for our potential impact on the Indians. We had come to their country to learn from them. The burden was on us to look for clues and act accordingly. We had to realize that we might wish to be loud, informal, and inquisitive, but that for some people, that behavior might be difficult to accept. I erred on the conservative side, causing some students to feel that I was rigid and overly cautious. Sometimes they were right; many times Indians enjoyed those outgoing characteristics and qualities. Sometimes the Gujarat Vidyapith standards were different from those of other Indians.

The role required a constant gauging of the situation, looking out for assumptions that American students were making, following the group dynamics, deciding whether to broach a subject or to let it come up on its own. I needed both to be close to them and to keep a distance. I needed to accept them totally and also to challenge them.

I think the most difficult aspect for me was being constantly engaged. We lived with each other day and night until the homestays. School never ended. I had my own room, but I did not have much of an outside friendship circle. It was difficult to feel any kind of personal identity outside the role of academic director—broad-ranging as that might be. Even more important, however, I craved colleagues with whom I could discuss the questions and dilemmas that I was facing. This lack was exhausting and contributed to the intensity of the experience. A sense of humor was the absolutely essential ingredient that kept me going.

The second semester predictably went much better. The Vidyapith staff knew me and I knew them. I had a better idea of whom to invite to lecture and which organizations to visit. I anticipated students' reactions and was better able to explain difficulties. I found that one of the ways I could be most helpful to students was to meet with them individually; it was part of being constantly involved. I was always available to them to discuss their ISP project, some other aspect of their work, their relationships within the group, or their worries about friends and family at home. I felt I was able to be more helpful to some students than to others.

What were my "ahas" as academic director? What did I learn about myself, my students and this process? I learned again that one is never teaching any more or less than oneself. I was a model of how to get along in this particular situation, sometimes a successful one who managed to communicate, enjoy, and stay true to myself and sometimes less successful when my self-doubts clouded my ability to respond.

I learned that I needed to allow the students the space to complain, bad-mouth, and express their negative feelings about the host culture. This process allowed them to let off steam and articulate sometimes unidentified frustrations. It often took a humorous turn when they realized how seriously they had taken conditions. Once expressed, there was much more of a chance to move on than if they hadn't vented these feelings. It took me a little while to feel comfortable with this process, however.

At one time I thought the key element to making cross-cultural study successful was to be sure that the heart and head were combined in the study; that, in fact, the heart should lead the way, directing the way to subject matter, contacts, and experiences. I now feel, after our experience at the Gujarat Vidyapith, that an additional important element is awareness. If the students could be aware of their reactions and feelings, ask why, and learn to bear witness during the process, they would then be equipped to cope with experiences over which they were not always in control.

How could I best help students make the most out of difficult situations? How could I encourage them to go beyond their uncomfortable dislike for the food, their annoyance with subservience, their judgments of the less-than-Gandhian attitudes of the faculty at the Vidyapith? How could I guide them towards accepting their feelings and going beyond to ask why, towards understanding and remaining open rather than writing their feelings off? How could I encourage students to stay in the messy confusion of trying to figure out their values, which were being challenged, rather than to give up and return to an "I'm right, and they're wrong" posture?

The students learned to live in India by using trial-and-error methods. I did the same in answering the above questions. As best I could I modeled ways of interpreting difficulties; I attempted to remain calm or appropriately indignant, respectful but persevering. I also asked them questions when they raised difficulties, encouraging them to speak specifically to the issue that was beneath the judgment.

I was there to listen, probe, and challenge. I could act as a sounding board, a buffer, and an interpreter. I was there, hopefully, as an advocate for them. I saw my most fulfilling work to be one of critical encouragement and affirmation, of being a bellows for that spark within. The most important component, though, was simply realizing that they were teaching themselves.

At the end of both semesters, I found myself deeply moved as I listened to them talk about what they had learned, their insights, and their gained wisdom. There was further to go. And, at the same time, they really had changed. I had witnessed what I consider to be the magic of transformation. I was proud of them for coming on this trip, for undergoing constant scrutiny when out on the streets, living in very different conditions from those at home, working with their own barriers and limitations. I found it terribly gratifying that they took the semester so seriously. They had invested a lot. I'm reminded of what Robert Kegan said as he watched his young daughter:

> Being in another person's presence while she so honestly labors in an astonishingly intimate activity—the activity of making sense—is somehow very touching.[3]

I found it so.

APPENDIX 2

Program and Course Objectives

Educational Objectives of the Program for Students

1. To gain a broad and basic understanding of contemporary Indian society with a special focus on the impact of Gandhi's life and thought in areas of politics, education, development, and social change.

2. To develop the ability to communicate with members of the host country through the use of the Gujarati language and the understanding of nonverbal clues, enabling students to more completely understand the cultural contexts within which they are working and living.

3. To acquire cross-cultural and field research skills to enter deeply and sensitively into the Indian culture while developing an awareness applicable to any cross-cultural experience.

4. To develop responsibility for self-motivated learning, awareness of individual learning style, and the capacity to design and implement an in-depth, independent study project.

5. To develop an increased understanding and respect for different ways of life and thought and to take responsibility for living in an interdependent world.

Gujarati Language

1. To develop basic Gujarati conversational skills.

2. To build a grammatical foundation.

3. To work on pronunciation and verbal expression.

4. To learn to understand nonverbal communication.

5. To become familiar with Gujarati script.

Life and Culture Seminar

1. To explore Indian culture through five major areas of inquiry: (a) Gandhian philosophy, (b) arts and religion, (c) history, politics, and economics, (d) social anthropology, and (e) rural development and modernization.

2. To better understand Gandhi and Gandhism since Independence.

3. Through homestay experience, scheduled activities, and group discussions, to have opportunities to interact sensitively and responsibly with Indians and thereby to begin to understand specific attitudes, behaviors, and practices found in some parts of Indian culture.

4. To take on academic and social responsibilities in order to learn to function competently and independently in another culture.

5. To further self-understanding through participation in another culture.

Methods and Techniques of Field Study

1. To become aware of experiential learning processes outside the institutional structure and to develop self-motivated learning skills.

2. To learn methods that are necessary to conduct an

independent study project in a foreign setting and to learn to analyze and report results.

3. To learn to use primary sources.

4. To choose an ISP topic and methodology that is realistically within the constraints of time and resources, yet which challenges one to push beyond these limits.

Independent Study Project

1. To design a study project which is based on field-oriented data gathering.

2. To learn to work closely with the project advisor and other resources available in the culture.

3. To convey succinctly the importance of the project, both in written and oral presentations.

NOTES

Chapter One: The Beginning

1. School for International Training 1984-1985 College Semester Abroad Brochure, Brattleboro, VT.

2. See appendix 2 for course objectives.

3. Kalvero Oberg, *Readings in Intercultural Communication*, Vol. II, David S. Hoopes ed. (Washington D.C.: Society for Intercultural Education Training and Research, 1972).

4. Kalvero Oberg, "Culture Shock and the Problems of Adjustment to New Cultural Environments"; talk given at the Women's Club of Rio de Janeiro, date unknown.

5. Peter S. Adler, "Culture Shock and the Cross-Cultural Learning Experience" (Brattleboro, VT: School for International Training, date and origin unknown).

6. For an in-depth discussion of the pull between safety and risk, see Abraham Maslow, *Toward a Psychology of Being*, Part 2, "Growth and Motivation" (New York: Van Nostrand Reinhold Co., Inc., 1968), p. 67.

7. Robert Kegan, *The Evolving Self* (Cambridge: Harvard University Press, 1982), p. 81.

8. Kohls offers a useful definition: "An integrated system of learned behavior patterns that are characteristic of the members of any given society. Culture refers to the way of life of particular groups of people. It includes everything that a group of people thinks, says, does, and makes its customs, language, material artifacts and shared systems of attitudes and feelings. Culture is learned and transmitted from generation to generation." L. Robert Kohls, *Survival Kit for Overseas Living* (Yarmouth, ME: Intercultural Press Inc., 1984), p. 17.

9. Kegan, p. 39.

10. Theodore Gochenour and Anne Janeway, "Seven Concepts in Cross-Cultural Interaction," in *Beyond Experience*, Donald Batchelder and Elizabeth G. Warner eds. (Brattleboro, VT: The Experiment Press, 1977), p. 16.

11. Gochenour and Janeway, p. 16.

12. Edward T. Hall, *The Silent Language* (Garden City, NY: Anchor/Doubleday, 1973), p. 28.

13. When Geoff returned to Sadra four months later, it took him an hour and a half to get from the bus stop to the Vidyapith, usually a ten-minute walk. All along the way he was called into villagers' homes to have tea, a glass of water, some biscuits; he was very much welcomed back into town.

14. David S. Hoopes, "Intercultural Communication Concepts and the Psychology of Intercultural Experience," in *Multicultural Education: A Cross-Cultural Training Approach*, Margaret D. Pusch ed. (Yarmouth, ME: Intercultural Press Inc., 1979), p. 23.

15. Ruth Benedict, *Patterns of Culture* (New York: New American Library, 1934), p. 33.

16. Kohls, p. 54.

17. Sri Nisargadatta Maharaj, *I Am That: Talks with Sri Nisargadatta Maharaj*, Sudhakar S. Dikshit ed. (Durham, NC: Acorn Press, 1982), p. vi.

Chapter Two: Sinking In

1. Quoted in Kegan, p. 11.

2. Gochenour and Janeway, p. 19.

3. Paul Rabinow, *Reflections on Fieldwork in Morocco* (Rowley, MA: Newbury House Publishers, 1979), p. 154.

4. Edward Stewart, "American Assumptions and Values: Orientation to Action," in *Toward Internationalism*, Elise C. Smith and Louise Fiber Luce eds.(Rowley, MA: Newbury House Publishers, 1979), p. 1.

5. Robert N. Bellah, Richard Madsen, William M. Sullivan, Ann Swindler, Steven M. Tipton, *Habits of the Heart* (Berkeley: University of California Press, 1985), p. 23.

6. Gochenour and Janeway, p. 18.

Chapter Three: Independence and Integration

1. Benedict, p. 2.

2. Donald Batchelder, "The Drop-Off," in *Beyond Experience*, Batchelder and Warner eds., p. 115.

3. Donald Batchelder, "The Green Banana," in *Beyond Experience,* Batchelder and Warner eds., p. 138.

4. Gordon Murray, "The Inner Side of Cross-Cultural Learning," in Batchelder and Warner, p. 171.

5. Penny is expressing an American value. She had found a shifting dynamics in Indian society. Although women have newfound legal rights, their duty is still to put husband and family before self. It's likely that their "needs and desires" will always include some relationship to husband, family, caste, and religion. We have much to learn from Indian women as they continue to explore the tensions between familial responsibility and individual freedom.

6. Kegan uses this expression throughout his book, *The Evolving Self*, starting on p. 11.

Chapter Four: Homestays

1. Gochenour and Janeway, p. 21.

2. Hoopes, in "Intercultural Communication Concepts and the Psychology of Intercultural Experience," in *Multicultural Education: A Cross Cultural Training Approach*, Pusch, ed., p. 19.

Chapter Five: Evaluation

1. Robert G. Hanvey, "Cross-Cultural Awareness," in *Toward Internationalism*, Smith and Luce, p. 51.

2. Batchelder and Warner, p. 143.

3. In the end we compromised. He said he should either get a "C" for not doing the assignment well and ending up writing a library research paper, or he should get an "A" for venturing off and trying. I decided to give him a "B" because I recognized both arguments and because he realized how his expectations had limited his investigation.

Chapter Six: Implications

1. Maslow, *Toward a Psychology of Being*, p. 212.

2. Maslow, "Defense and Growth."

3. Quoted by Robert G. Hanvey in "Cross-Cultural Awareness," in Smith and Luce, p. 48.

4. Kegan, p. 17.

5. Bellah et al., *Habits of the Heart*, p. 295.

6. Bellah et al., pp. 295-96.

7. Elenore Smith Bowen talks about this issue strongly in her novel, *Return to Laughter* (Garden City, NY: Natural History Library Edition, 1964), p. 121.

8. Maslow comments, "We may not be aware when we perceive in a need-determined way. But we certainly are aware of it when we ourselves are perceived in this way, e.g., simply as a money-giver, a food supplier.... When this happens we don't like it at all. We want to be taken for ourselves, as complete and whole individuals. We dislike being perceived as useful objects or as tools." p. 40.

9. Robert G. Hanvey, "Cross-Cultural Awareness," in Smith and Luce, p. 53.

10. Robert Boehm, *Notes on India* (Boston: South End Press, 1980).

Appendix 1: Life of an Academic Director

1. Job description for academic director at the School for International Training, Brattleboro, VT.

2. Robert Kegan: "The two greatest yearnings of human life, I have suggested, may be the yearning for inclusion (to be welcomed in, next to, held, connected with, a part of) and the yearning for distinctness (to be autonomous, independent, to experience my own agency, the self-chosenness of my purposes). This shift from an overly integrated balance to an overly differentiated one is repeated later in life, usually in late adolescence or early adulthood." p. 143.

3. Kegan, p. 16.

BIBLIOGRAPHY

Adler, Peter S. "Beyond Cultural Identity: Reflections on Cultural and Multicultural Man." *Topics in Culture Learning 2* (1974).

_____. "Culture Shock and the Cross-Cultural Learning Experience." Available through School for International Training in Vermont. (Date unknown)

Ashton-Warner, Sylvia. *Teacher.* New York: Simon and Schuster, 1963.

Batchelder, Donald, and Warner, Elizabeth G. *Beyond Experience: The Experimental Approach to Cross-Cultural Education.* Brattleboro, VT: The Experiment Press, 1977.

Bellah, Robert N.; Madsen, Richard; Sullivan, William M.; Swindler, Ann; and Tipton, Steven M. *Habits of the Heart: Individualism and Commitment.* Berkeley: University of California Press, 1985.

Benedict, Ruth. *Patterns of Culture.* New York: New American Library, 1934.

Boehm, Robert. *Notes on India.* Boston: South End Press, 1980.

Bowen, Elenore Smith. *Return to Laughter.* Garden City, NY: National History Library Edition, 1964.

Brislin, Richard W., and Van Buren, IV, H. "Can They Go Home Again?" Culture Learning Institute, East-West Center, Honolulu (Spring 1974).

Casse, Pierre. *Training for the Cross-Cultural Mind.* Washington, DC: Society for Intercultural Education, Training and Research, 1979.

"Coming Home Again." Center for International and Area Studies, Brigham Young University, Provo, Utah, 1980.

Crowther, Geoff; Prakash, A. Raj; and Wheeler, Tony. *India—A Travel Survival Kit.* Victoria, Australia: Lonely Planet Publications, 1981.

Dass, Ram, and Gorman, Paul. *How Can I Help?* New York: Alfred A. Knopf, 1985.

Dikshit, Sudhakar S. *I Am That: Talks with Sri Nisargadatta Maharaj.* Durham, NC: Acorn Press, 1982.

Erikson, Erik H. *Adulthood.* New York: W.W. Norton & Co., 1978.

_____. *Identity, Youth and Crisis.* New York: W.W. Norton & Co., 1968.

_____. *Identity and the Life Cycle.* New York: W.W. Norton & Co., 1980.

Gandhi, Mohandas K. *An Autobiography: The Story of My Experiments with Truth.* Boston: Beacon Press, 1957.

Gochenour, Theodore, and Janeway, Anne. "Seven Concepts in Cross-Cultural Interaction." In *Beyond Experience.* Brattleboro, VT: The Experiment Press, 1977.

Hall, Edward T. *The Hidden Dimension.* New York: Doubleday & Co., Inc., 1966.

_____. *The Silent Language*. Garden City, NY: Anchor/Doubleday, 1973.

Hanvey, Robert G. "Cross-Cultural Awareness." In *Toward Internationalism*, edited by Elise C. Smith and Louise Fiber Luce. Rowley, MA: Newbury House Publishers, 1979.

Hoopes, David S. "Intercultural Communication Concepts and the Psychology of Intercultural Experience." In *Multicultural Education: A Cross-Cultural Training Approach*, edited by Margaret D. Pusch. Yarmouth, ME: Intercultural Press Inc., 1979.

Hoopes, David S. *Readings in Intercultural Communication, Vol. II*. Washington, DC: Society for Intercultural Education, Training, and Research, 1972.

Kegan, Robert. *The Evolving Self*. Cambridge, MA: Harvard University Press, 1982.

Kohls, L. Robert *Survival Kit for Overseas Living*. Yarmouth, ME: Intercultural Press Inc., 1984.

Krishnamurti, J. *Letters to the Schools*. Madras, India: Krishnamurti Foundation India, 1981.

Maslow, Abraham H. *Toward a Psychology of Being*. New York: Van Nostrand Reinhold Co., Inc., 1968.

Murray, Gordon. "The Inner Side of Cross-Cultural Learning." In *Beyond Experience*, edited by Donald Batchelder and Elizabeth Warner. Brattleboro, VT: The Experiment Press, 1977.

National Association for Foreign Student Affairs. *Learning Across Cultures*. Intercultural Communication and International Educational Exchange. Washington, DC: National Association for Foreign Student Affairs, 1981.

Pusch, Margaret D., ed. *Multicultural Education: A Cross-Cultural Training Approach*. Yarmouth, ME: Intercultural Press Inc., 1979.

Rabinow, Paul. *Reflections on Fieldwork in Morocco*. Rowley, MA: Newbury House Publishers, 1977.

Smith, Elise C., and Luce, Louise Fiber, eds. *Toward Internationalism: Readings in Cross-Cultural Communication*. Rowley, MA: Newbury House Publishers, 1979.

Staley, John. *People in Development: A Trainer's Manual for Groups*. Bangalore, India: SEARCH, 1982.

Stewart, Edward. "American Assumptions and Values: Orientation to Action." In *Toward Internationalism*, edited by Elise C. Smith and Louise Fiber Luce. Rowley, MA: Newbury House Publishers, 1979.

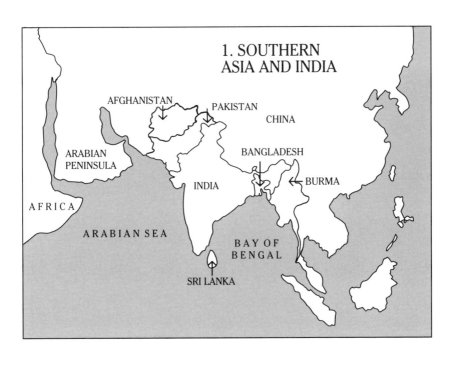

1. SOUTHERN ASIA AND INDIA

AFGHANISTAN

PAKISTAN

CHINA

ARABIAN PENINSULA

BANGLADESH

INDIA

BURMA

AFRICA

ARABIAN SEA

BAY OF BENGAL

SRI LANKA

2. THE STATES OF INDIA

Jammu & Kashmir

Himachal Pradesh

Punjab

Haryana

DELHI

Rajasthan

Gujurat

Uttar Pradesh

Madhya Pradesh

Bihar

West Bengal

Sikkim

Maharashtra

Orissa

Andhra Pradesh

GOA

Karnataka

Tamil Nadu

Kerala

1 Meghalaya
2 Assam
3 Arunachal Pradesh
4 Nagaland
5 Manipur
6 Mizoram
7 Tripura

Andaman & Nicobar Islands

157

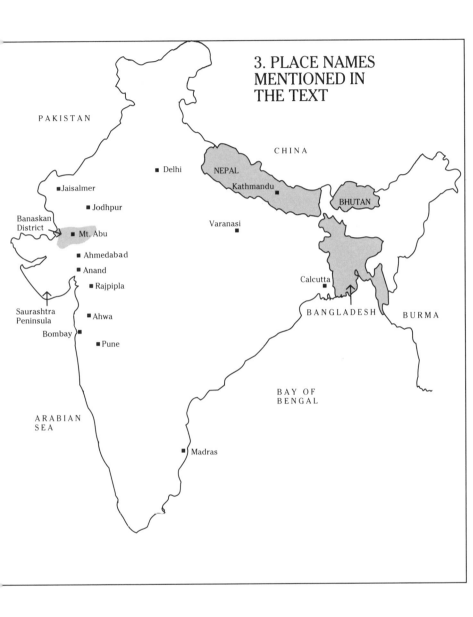

3. PLACE NAMES
MENTIONED IN
THE TEXT

PAKISTAN

CHINA

■ Delhi

NEPAL

Kathmandu

BHUTAN

■Jaisalmer

■ Jodhpur

Banaskan
District

Varanasi
■

■ Mt. Abu

■ Ahmedabad

■ Anand

Calcutta
■

■ Rajpipla

Saurashtra
Peninsula

BANGLADESH

BURMA

■ Ahwa

Bombay ■

■ Pune

BAY OF
BENGAL

ARABIAN
SEA

■ Madras